KEEPERS OF THE PAST

Keepers
of the Past

Edited by
Clifford L. Lord

THE UNIVERSITY OF NORTH CAROLINA PRESS
CHAPEL HILL

Copyright © 1965 by
The University of North Carolina Press

Manufactured in the United States of America
Library of Congress Catalog Card Number 65-23141

PRINTED BY THE SEEMAN PRINTERY, DURHAM, N. C.

Contents

By Way of Background   3
   By Clifford L. Lord

I. THE HISTORICAL SOCIETY

Jeremy Belknap   19
   By Stephen T. Riley

John Pintard   30
   By James J. Heslin

Lyman Copeland Draper   40
   By Larry Gara

Reuben Gold Thwaites   53
   By Clifford L. Lord

Dixon Ryan Fox   67
   By John Allen Krout

II. THE PUBLIC ARCHIVE

John Franklin Jameson   81
   By David D. Van Tassel

Thomas McAdory Owen, Sr.   97
   By James F. Doster

Robert Digges Wimberly Connor   109
   By Hugh T. Lefler

Contents

III. THE HISTORICAL MUSEUM

George Brown Goode   127
    By G. Carroll Lindsay

Edgar Lee Hewett   141
    By James Taylor Forrest

George Francis Dow   157
    By Charles B. Hosmer, Jr.

IV. THE SPECIAL COLLECTION

Henry Edwards Huntington   169
    By John E. Pomfret

Bella C. Landauer   180
    By James J. Heslin

V. THE HISTORIC SITE

Ann Pamela Cunningham   193
    By Charles B. Hosmer, Jr.

Adina De Zavala   203
    By L. Robert Ables

William Sumner Appleton   215
    By Bertram K. Little

Stephen Hyatt Pelham Pell   223
    By Edward P. Hamilton

John D. Rockefeller, Jr.   232
    By Fairfield Osborn

The Authors   239

KEEPERS OF THE PAST

By Way of Background
by Clifford L. Lord

Though historic preservation in the United States—covering in its broadest sense manuscripts and archives, artifacts, sites, and structures—can be traced fitfully to early colonial days, in a formal organized sense it may be said to date from the early days of the republic when Jeremy Belknap launched the Massachusetts Historical Society on its distinguished career. Thereafter, its development is one of the fascinating yet strangely neglected sectors of American intellectual history. Today, nearly 175 years later, almost every state has at least one statewide historical society and some have more; almost every county and quite a few hamlets are organized in support of Clio; national and state archives are supplemented by corporate archives and a growing number of county and municipal archives; almost every town cherishes at least one more or less historic building, and several of our major restorations attract better than a million visitors a year. Expenditures, financed partly from contributions, partly from earnings, partly from tax-dollars, surely approximate fifty million dollars a year.

Here is a field of endeavor that clearly reflects and responds to the major developments of American history. It could not have grown to its present proportions except in an affluent and highly mobile society, or in a society where the avocational enthusiasm of the middle-aged could be supplemented by the enthusiasm and support of many oldsters. Because it is something most people *could* do without if they had to, it has been singularly responsive to depressions—the slaughter of local historical societies during the Great Depression was enormous. It has been singularly responsive to patriotic enthusiasm; historical societies increased in number and site preservation began as nationalism hit its stride in the so-called Middle Period of the nineteenth century and rose again with the impact of the Centennial of Independence in 1876. Such activities fell off drastically, but temporarily, under the demands for manpower, time, and money during World War II, and they rose to new heights in the days of the Cold War when for the first time America and its accepted way of life faced a powerful, continuing, subverting, hostile challenge. It has been affected by the waves of immigration from Europe in the nineteenth and early twentieth centuries. As is true of any continuingly important segment of our economy or society, the history of historical organizations can be understood only in terms of the over-all history of the country; conversely, in a certain sense the history of the country could be taught and understood in terms of the history of its historical organizations. Yet the field has been largely neglected.

Indeed, the history of the movement today can barely be sketched. The historical society, beginning in Massachusetts in 1791, has thrice been surveyed, once by the Bureau of Education in connection with the Centennial of Independence,[1] then for the period before 1860 by Leslie Dunlap in 1944,[2] and again in 1959 by the American Association for State and Local History.[3] It was even more recently looked at in a somewhat less comprehensive fashion by Walter Muir Whitehill during his safaris about the hinterlands in search of material for his *Independent Historical Societies*.[4] Histories of the Massachusetts,

By Way of Background

New-York, Pennsylvania, Chicago, and Missouri State societies as well as the Essex Institute have been published in book form. Most others have been covered in whole or in part by various articles and occasional mimeographed publications.[5] Biographies of such leaders in the field as Isaiah Thomas, Lyman Copeland Draper, and Alexander Wall have been printed, and memorial volumes published by the respective societies cover the lives and contributions of many others.

The chapters of the first half of Dunlap's survey of societies founded before 1860 suggest the European origin of the historical society with somewhat greater anatomical precision than did Robert Seton.[6] Dunlap also suggests the relationship, in the founding of historical societies, among the paucity of library resources in most of the country throughout most of the nineteenth century, the stimulus of patriotism, a recognition in a few quarters of the importance of preserving old records, and a certain amount of self-serving.

It is clear from Dunlap's state-by-state surveys of American historical societies and from the tables at the end of the 1876 survey by the Bureau of Education—though there are startling variations between the two in several instances—that the first appreciable number of societies, were founded in the 1820's. In that decade, Maine, New Hampshire, Connecticut, and Rhode Island joined Massachusetts in New England; Pennsylvania, Tennessee, Illinois, and Michigan were organized. So, too, was one of the first county societies, that of Worcester, Massachusetts, and one of the early patriotic societies, the Pilgrim Society. Ohio was chartered but not organized. Aside from Tennessee (the Antiquarian Society), the South was slower to make plans: Virginia organized in 1831, Louisiana in 1835, Kentucky in 1838, Georgia in 1839, North Carolina in 1844 (though chartered eleven years earlier). By mid-century, the states east of the Mississippi were, with few exceptions, organized, and local

{5}

societies were blossoming widely, especially in Massachusetts and Ohio.

The historical and antiquarian societies were quickly joined by old settlers' and pioneers' organizations, particularly in the West. Patriotic groups increased in number, and as one nationality group after another became increasingly absorbed into the main stream of American culture, historical societies based on nationality came into being, in no small part to perpetuate the memory and the culture of the old country: Germans and Irish to start with, then—later—the Norwegians, the Swiss, and later still, the Italians and others.

A major change in the nature of the historical society came with the Progressive Era. The same forces that attacked trusts, monopolies, and corruption; pushed more and more authority into the hands of the people through the direct primary, the direct election of senators, the short ballot, the initiative, referendum, and recall; brought the Social Gospel to the fore in the theology of the land; and—also a sign of increasing affluence —raised high school attendance to new heights, brought major new content to the historical society. Under the dynamic leadership of Reuben Gold Thwaites, the Wisconsin society became the first great progressive historical society, recognizing its responsibilities in public education (museum, sites and markers, centennials and pageants, work with the schools, serving the public as well as the scholar), and launching a program whose impact is still visible throughout the movement.

The development of the automobile made possible the rapid growth of shrines and sites; the emancipation of women brought them to new posts of power and influence in historical organizations; the progress of science and medicine brought more elderly people to the rolls of active membership; the growing gross national product brought more funds, both public and private, to this type of activity. And the progressive approach was

By Way of Background

pushed with vigor and effectiveness by the American Association for State and Local History after its founding in 1940.

While the chief activities of the early societies centered on the library and on the publication of papers and documents, most of them also had a larger or smaller "cabinet of curiosities." Begun in the days before the camera had been perfected, these cabinets unquestionably served a useful educational function. Items from the Fiji Islands or from Micronesia vied with Egyptian mummies and two-headed calves to intrigue the visitor and to stir curiosity. Contacts with the outside world were few for most people in those days, and the artifact from a strange part of the world was a welcome interest-arouser. But the photograph brought the rest of the world much closer to a man's home. The advent of the major museum decreased greatly the significance of the smaller cabinet. The transition was from the collections of the Essex Institute or the New-York Historical Society, on the one hand, and P. T. Barnum's sideshows, on the other, to the Museum of Natural History (New York) or the Smithsonian. Slowly, the cabinet of curiosities lost its impact. Reform came in weeding out collections, selective collecting policies, and modern display methods. The modern historical museum began to evolve gradually from the cabinet early in the twentieth century. The process was slow, almost glacial, and the pace varied from institution to institution, but it came with gathering momentum in the 1940's.

Old records were, of course, of basic importance in the field of preservation. Bauer[7] and others have noted the numerous instances in which the governments of the colonies and the early states moved for the better care of important government documents: Massachusetts as early as 1639 but more effectively in 1836; Maryland in 1723 and 1740; New Jersey in 1784; New Hampshire and Georgia in 1810.

Preservation through publication of selected records attracted considerable attention in the nineteenth century (as it has again in recent years). The compilation and publication of the two volume *Historical Collections* (1792, 1794) by Ebenezer Hazard set the precedent. There followed Jared Sparks's four major series in 38 volumes; the publication of *American State Papers* (1789-1838) in 38 volumes; Peter Force's *American Archives* (1837-53) in 9 volumes; the government's printing of the *Annals of Congress* (1834-56); *Foreign Relations* beginning in 1861; the *Rebellion Records* (1880 in 130 volumes).

But publication was usually highly selective, and selection came under more and more condemnation by the German trained Ph.D.'s of the last quarter of the nineteenth century. In addition, publication was relatively expensive, and it could not be the complete answer to the preservation of important records. The action of Massachusetts to establish a Commissioner of Public Records in 1884 and of Pennsylvania the following year to provide for classification and binding of old records and the transfer of manuscript materials to the state library for preservation and reference, set a new trend.

A federal program began to emerge also. In 1877, a presidential commission joined the small but growing public outcry for fireproof buildings for public records, specifically recommending such a building for the federal government. In 1889, Congress authorized the destruction of "useless" records. In 1903, as the effective work of the American Historical Association in the promotion of modern state and federal archival programs was beginning to be felt, Congress authorized the transfer to the Library of Congress of records of special value.

Three years earlier the American Historical Association had established the Public Archives Commission, begun the surveys of state archives, and, through the Carnegie Institution of Washington, started a survey of government archives in Washington. At the same time, beginning with a resolution in 1901 calling for a national hall of records, the association maintained pressure for an effective federal program. Progress was interrupted by

By Way of Background

World War I after Congress had called for an inspection of European facilities before making firm plans for an archival establishment. With the support of the American Legion and the Hearst papers, the association finally persuaded Congress in 1926 to authorize the erection of the National Archives building, which was opened in 1934.

From the turn-of-the-century ferment in the American Historical Association came the Conference on Historical Societies (1907) which became the American Association for State and Local History (1940), and the Conference of Archivists (1909) which became the Society of American Archivists (1937). And after the establishment of the National Archives under the act of that name of June 19, 1934, came the long controversy between the records management experts and the archivists; the huge inventorying projects of the Historical Records Survey, the Survey of Federal Archives outside the District of Columbia, and the Court Records Survey; the establishment of the presidential libraries beginning with Hyde Park under the Act of July 18, 1939, and the later act of August 12, 1955. The National Historical Publications Commission, established under the Archives Act of 1934, was activated in 1950 and revived the nineteenth-century program of publishing series of papers, now those of individuals and more catholic than selective in content.

The preservation of historic buildings and sites also came in for early attention. The slaughter was substantial; the recorded efforts to fight "progress" in the early years of the nineteenth century are few. Undoubtedly, the number of unsuccessful crusades, such as those of the Rhode Island Historical Society in 1834 to save the Coddington House or that to save the Russell House at Branford, Connecticut, where Yale College was started, is legion if largely unknown. The first recorded success came at Newburgh, New York, where the failure to raise private funds to preserve Hasbrouck House (Washington's Headquarters) led to legislative action sponsored by Andrew Caldwell

Keepers of the Past

and Governor Hamilton Fish. Tennessee followed with the purchase in 1856 of Andrew Jackson's Hermitage, though this was almost lost when the federal government failed to accept the property as a site for a southern branch of the U.S. Military Academy. That same year, Washington's presidential residence in New York was torn down, a fate suffered by the John Hancock House in Boston a few years later.

Preservation gathered momentum after the Civil War. The final success of the long-drawn-out fight to save Mount Vernon; the founding of effective preservation societies in Virginia, the District of Columbia, New York, and New England; the renaissance of the Spanish missions of the Southwest; the work of the patriotic and hereditary societies; the preservation by the Interior Department of many Indian pueblos; the beginnings of historical society interest in saving historic buildings—all these combined to bring considerable success by 1920.[8] The mid-twenties unveiled a new phase of the movement with the multi-million dollar intervention of the Rockefellers in the reconstruction and restoration of Colonial Williamsburg and the transplantation of the outdoor museum, pioneered by Vaselius, to the American scene. The depression brought relief labor to projects ranging from the restoration of New Salem to that of the local historic home, and added the stimulus of the Historic American Buildings Survey to the already stirring interest of the American Institute of Architects. Since World War II, the movement has gained increasing momentum until one wag recently suggested that the nation was suffering from an "edifice complex." Since World War II, the advent of public housing programs, urban renewal, and expressways has brought the problem of old building preservation to the fore in one city after another with new urgency, with new promise of respect for the importance of such reminders of the past, and with new tools, such as historic zoning, with which to work.

To single out the key figures in these many sided develop-

By Way of Background

ments is to invite criticism and seemingly to slight other unquestionably worthy leaders. However, the attempt has been made, concentrating on people who, in this field, made notable things happen. No living person has been included as a subject in the following biographical sketches.

The historical society is greatly indebted to its two progenitors in this country: the Reverend Jeremy Belknap and John Pintard, collaborators in launching the first two societies. To the type of society the former founded, Lyman Copeland Draper in Wisconsin added annual state appropriations and demonstrated how to build a great library without a major benefactor. And on this foundation, Reuben Gold Thwaites built the first of the great democratic progressive societies, introducing the function of public education as the second great purpose of the historical society. Dixon Ryan Fox combined scholarship, the progressive society, and the outdoor museum in the New York State Historical Association which he guided for thirteen years.

The historical museum, as a part of the museum world in general, is indebted to G. Brown Goode, noted ichthyologist, who crusaded within the American Historical Association and elsewhere for the museum as a teaching device, as an educational vehicle of great significance. Preaching the combination of study collections for the scholar and attractive story-telling exhibits for the public, he made a notable contribution to the development of the modern museum, historical and otherwise. And among special contributors to the modern museum display, George Francis Dow, the pioneer in this country of the small-scale diorama, has been singled out for inclusion. This is, above all, a story-telling device, the objects scaled down to where they can be encompassed in a small display, yet authentic in detail. Before the progressive revolution in which Thwaites added popular education to the functions of the historical society, and greeted the museum as the equal of the public library as a device of public education, such dioramas would, in all probability, have received short shrift from the historical museum director. Dow had forerunners and many copiers, but his work is of cardinal importance in this area of historical display.

In the preservation of public records, one conceivably could go back at least to Josiah Quincy or take one of the early preservers-by-selective-publication such as Ebenezer Hazard or Jared Sparks or Peter Force. Instead, three figures in the emergence of the professional archivist were chosen. Any story of records' preservation would be hopelessly prejudiced without the inclusion of John Franklin Jameson, who did so much in the late nineteenth and early twentieth century in archives, European transcripts, and documentary publication, and who is unquestionably more responsible than any other single individual for the establishment of the national archives. In addition, two twentieth-century figures were tapped: Thomas M. Owen, Sr., who created and developed in Alabama the first state department of archives and history and contributed greatly to the movement for such state agencies; and his contemporary, R. D. W. Connor, who built the North Carolina department of archives and history into a broader vehicle of preservation and dissemination and went on to become the first archivist of the United States. From both positions, he exercised considerable influence.

Similarly, the preservation and restoration of historic sites abounds with important figures. Selected for inclusion are: Ann Pamela Cunningham, the single-minded, indefatigable invalid who saved Mount Vernon; the dynamic, dictatorial, controversial Adina De Zavala who won the second battle of the Alamo; William Sumner Appleton, whose Society for the Preservation of New England Antiquities—much like Andrew H. Green's American Scenic and Historic Preservation Society in New York—deserves credit for much of the preservation work in New England in the first quarter of the twentieth century, a man who pioneered the concept in this country of saving the structure, even if it were used for utilitarian function. In New

By Way of Background

Mexico, the remarkable Dr. Edgar Hewett was simultaneously putting together a formidable chain of pueblos and the Spanish governor's palace for the state museum. And at Ticonderoga, New York, Stephen H. P. Pell, as head of a family enterprise and operating largely on an entrepreneurial basis, was bringing Fort Ticonderoga close to its original formidability. John D. Rockefeller, Jr., because he transformed the Reverend W. A. R. Goodwin's very modest proposal for Williamsburg into the vision of what Williamsburg could be made, and because of the tremendous influence of the project thus launched, is central to any account of the large-scale restoration work that bulks so large in the movement in the second quarter of the twentieth century.

To historical society, library and museum, the special collector has brought great riches, sometimes by gift or bequest, sometimes by working actively during his lifetime with the institution of his choice. He has also opened up one new field of collecting after another and, in so doing, has focused attention on its utility to social, cultural, and, sometimes, economic history. The collectors are legion, and selectivity here is particularly fraught with subjective perils. Our representatives are Henry E. Huntington, railroad magnate and capitalist, whose collecting hobby spawned what became the great Huntington Library; and Bella Landauer who recognized the importance of the hallmarks of retailing— the card, the ad, the label, the package—and presented her collection to the New-York Historical Society. Plans to include other key figures among such collectors were reluctantly abandoned, but surely two merit mention in this preface: Charles Messer Stow, for many years the distinguished antiques editor of the *New York Sun,* not so much a collector himself but an encourager of collectors of the decorative arts through his column, and the fosterer of the industrial and home arts through the work of the Early American Industries Association in which he was long a key figure; and Herbert A. Kellar, collector of the records and implements of agricultural history through extended service with the McCormick Historical Association (Chicago) and, in the latter years of his life, with the State Historical Society of Wisconsin.

In the following pages, the authors have tried to indicate not only what these people did in the broad field of preservation and what they contributed to the onward march of the movement, but what sort of people they were. Historically, most of the people involved in historical societies, museums, and sites have been amateurs, using this as an avocation, a hobby, an outlet, but earning their living by other means. Some were able, some were not so able; some were devoted, some not so devoted. But they gave unstintingly of their time and effort and money. Most of those included in this volume are amateurs in this sense. Increasingly, the professional, the man who earns his living in this particular field or some phase of it, has come into the picture. There were few before the Civil War, slowly but surely increasing in number as the economy grew, wealth increased, and both government and private sources became increasingly available to support projects of the sort to which this book addresses itself. Today, professionals are almost dominant in historical society work at the state level, in archives, in museums, and in sites, though the army of volunteers is still, and hopefully always will be, legion. The professionals in this book are few: Draper, Thwaites, Jameson, Owen, and Connor. Perhaps Fox, a professional historian though not a professional historical society man, and even Goode, an ichthyologist turned museum reformer, should be added. But the majority of the essays that follow are clearly about amateurs.

And a varied group they are. Writers, pedagogues, housewives, ministers, teachers, capitalists, and one who went to debtor's prison. Some prickly and cantankerous curmudgeons, some as smooth as silk. Men and women. Young and old. But all, in one form or another, devotees of Clio, and all of them people who got things done.

By Way of Background

As one more step in developing the story of those on whose shoulders those presently working these vineyards stand, the authors present these "Keepers of the Past."

NOTES

1. Department of the Interior, Bureau of Education, *Public Libraries in the United States of America, Their History, Condition, and Management* (Washington, D.C., 1876), pp. 312-77.
2. Leslie Dunlap, *Historical Societies in the United States, 1790-1860* (Madison, Wis., 1944).
3. Clement M. Silvestro and Richmond D. Williams, *A Look at Ourselves* (Madison, Wis., 1962).
4. Boston, Massachusetts, 1962.
5. The footnotes in Whitehill's *Independent Historical Societies* are the best single guide to these articles, though by no means all societies are covered, nor are all articles or even books cited for those societies which are mentioned. A more complete bibliography is being compiled in the office of the American Association for State and Local History.
6. Robert Seton, "The Origin of Historical Societies," *Records of the Catholic Historical Society of Philadelphia, 1884-1886* (1887), 1:52-58.
7. G. Philip Bauer, "Public Archives in the United States" in W. B. Hesseltine and D. R. McNeil, *In Support of Clio: Essays in Memory of Herbert A. Kellar* (Madison, Wis., 1955).
8. Charles Hosmer's *Presence of the Past* (National Trust for National Preservation, 1965), presents this story in detail.

I. The Historical Society

Jeremy Belknap
by Stephen T. Riley

The historical agency in the United States did not come into existence by itself, nor was it an idea conceived in the mind of one man alone. It was, rather, the product of many forces: the intellectual excitement that swept the country in the eighteenth century with its pervasive spirit of enquiry resulting in the formation of academies and societies; the budding sense of nationalism that stirred men's minds after the successful American Revolution and the adoption of the federal constitution; and the strong interest of many Americans in history that encouraged them to preserve for future generations the records of the glorious events they had experienced.

Although the idea of establishing an historical repository dedicated to the work of collecting, preserving, and publishing these records of a people was not unique to any one person, it can be said with certainty that it was one man who gave form and motion to this aspiration. That man was the Reverend Jeremy Belknap, minister of the Federal Street Church in Boston and chief founder in 1791 of the Massachusetts Historical Society, the first historical society in this country. For years, Belknap's name was largely unknown except to students of American literature or those interested in the origins of the historical society movement. Recently, however, there has been a growing awareness of his accomplishments in a variety of fields. It is now generally agreed that the United States had in Belknap one of its greatest boosters and that he worked untiringly to establish the institutions he thought would make the new nation strong.

Jeremy Belknap—he was christened Jeremiah but later shortened the name—was born in Boston on June 4, 1744, the son of Joseph and Sarah (Byles) Belknap. His father was a leather-dresser, and his mother was a niece of the Reverend Mather Byles, a noted clergyman and literary figure in his day. After a period of schooling at Lovell's, Jeremy entered Harvard on December 5, 1758, in his fifteenth year. In the interleaved almanacs that he began to keep at this time, he noted daily occurrences and such stirring events as the reduction of Louisbourg and Fort Duquesne and the expeditions against Crown Point and Ticonderoga. It is a wonder that he did not succumb to the lure of the drums as many of his fellows did. If he was tempted, he resisted manfully, for he managed to graduate with his class on July 21, 1762.

For a time Belknap taught school, thus following the normal course of young graduates preparing for the ministry. He kept the public grammar school at Milton, Massachusetts, until March, 1764, moving on in December to Portsmouth, New Hampshire, to keep the English school there. For a year or so, Belknap continued his teaching and studying, often tormented by self-doubts as to the genuineness of his call to the ministry. His doubts were resolved by an invitation from the parish at Dover on July 31, 1766. Belknap accepted, was ordained on February 18, 1767, and settled down to a pastorate of twenty not altogether happy years in this small New Hampshire town. The salary was not large, £100 per year with an initial allowance of £150 for a house, hardly enough to support his newly acquired wife, Ruth Eliot, daughter of Samuel Eliot, a bookseller in Boston, and the string of children that was soon to follow. Some

Jeremy Belknap

of the hardships of a country parson's wife are described by Belknap in the poem "The Pleasures of a Country Life," which he silently allowed to be attributed to Mrs. Belknap:

> Up in the morning I must rise
> Before I've time to rub my eyes.
> With half-pin'd gown, unbuckled shoe,
> I haste to milk my lowing cow.
> But, Oh! it makes my heart to ake,
> I have no bread till I can bake,
> And then, alas! it makes me sputter,
> For I must churn or have no butter.
> . . . .
> All summer long I toil & sweat
> Blister my hands, and scold & fret
> And when the summer's work is o'er,
> New toils arise from Autumn's store.
> . . . .
> Yet starch'd up folks that live in town,
> That lounge upon your beds till noon,
> That never tire yourselves with work,
> Unless with handling knife & fork,
> Come, see the sweets of country life,
> Display'd in Parson B———'s wife.

The first years of his ministry were busy ones. In addition to caring for his flock, Belknap soon found himself in demand as a public speaker. He was persuaded by his friend Captain Thomas W. Waldron of Dover to preach a sermon on military duty before Governor John Wentworth on November 10, 1772, on the occasion of a review of the Second Regiment of Foot. The sermon made a great impression on Governor Wentworth and resulted in the formation of a lasting friendship. When Belknap later sought material for his history of New Hampshire, Wentworth, although a Loyalist and a Crown official in Nova

Scotia, generously sent him the papers of his own administration in New Hampshire for study.

Some months earlier, Belknap had revealed his increasing interest in history to Waldron:

> You cannot help having observed in me an inquisitive disposition in historical matters. I find it so strong and powerful, and withal so increasing with my opportunities for gratifying it, that it has become a question with me, whether I might not fully indulge it, with a view to the benefit of my fellow-men, as well as for my own improvement. As it is natural for us to enquire into the ancient state and circumstances of the place of our own abode, and to entertain a peculiar fondness for such inquiries in preference to more foreign matters; so I have applied myself in some leisure hours (making it of late my principal amusement) to learn what I can from printed books and manuscripts and the information of aged and intelligent persons, of the former state and affairs of this town and province.

This interest lasted throughout his life and started him on such a successful search for early printed and manuscript records that his name has become a byword among collectors of historical materials. It also brought him into contact with such kindred spirits as the Reverend John Eliot (1754-1813), a founder of the Massachusetts Historical Society; Ebenezer Hazard (1744-1817), editor of historical records and postmaster general of the United States; John Pintard (1759-1844), founder of the New-York Historical Society; Benjamin Rush (1745-1813), physician and patriot; and a number of other antiquarians and writers. Fortunately, Belknap, isolated in his Dover parsonage much of the time, had to rely on correspondence with these friends. The record that remains gives us a good insight into the ideas that were being discussed by a very literate group of men in the last quarter of the eighteenth century.

Jeremy Belknap

But there were more immediate matters to capture Belknap's attention. Deeply disturbed by the widening breach between the colonies and Great Britain, he wasted no time in establishing his position. "If the principles that brought on the revolution, and established the house of Hanover on the throne, are just," he wrote, "then the supreme power of government lies in the people; consequently the people of America have a right to say who shall or who shall not govern them, then the claim exercised by the parliament is null and void." When the Boston Port Bill went into effect, he quickly put his pen at the service of the distressed inhabitants of that town. His address to the people of New Hampshire, signed "Amicus Patriae" and later printed in the *New Hampshire Gazette,* proved useful in persuading them to help with gifts of provisions and other necessaries. At one point, Belknap tried psychological warfare, writing an address to the officers of the British troops in Boston in September, 1774, designed to make them ashamed of their stand: "But, alas! gentlemen, though there be even a Miltiades or a Wolfe among you, the only honor you can derive from falling in the service on which you are now sent, will be to have it said that you were trampled in a gutter, or scalded with hot water from the ladle of some American Amazon, who may be celebrated in a two-penny ballad, long after your names are forgot." The address was intended for the *Massachusetts Spy,* but it did not appear there and may never have been printed.

News of the outbreak of the war reached Belknap when he was at the ferry midway between Portsmouth and Dover. He immediately set out for Boston to look after his parents but could not get into the town. After some days' wait in Cambridge, he finally effected the removal of his parents to Dover. In July, 1775, Belknap was chosen chaplain to the New Hampshire troops at Cambridge, but he declined to serve, pleading ill health, his duties in Dover, and family responsibilities. He did preach to the troops in October and recorded in his diary impressions

Keepers of the Past

of the military men he met in Cambridge. Belknap missed seeing General Washington at this time but developed a reverence for him that is evident in many of his letters and other writings.

For the remainder of the war, Belknap remained quietly in Dover, for the most part continuing his historical researches whenever he could take time from his regular duties. The pursuit of original sources fascinated him: "I am willing even to scrape a dunghill, if I may find a jewel at the bottom." He suffered many disappointments—discovering often that the records he sought had been lost by fire, carelessness, or intent. It must have galled him to receive uninterested answers to his queries concerning papers. One correspondent's reply to a request about Governor John Usher's manuscripts is described by Belknap as follows: "He knew of none, and it would take him months to look over the rubbish where they must be if in existence." Belknap was appalled by the lack of concern for public records and freely vented his feelings regarding the officials who were supposed to care for them, but he had successful days too. Writing to Hazard on June 10, 1783, from Boston, he said: "This day I set out homeward, with a grand acquisition since I have been here; viz., Governor Belcher's Letterbooks from 1732 to 1735. The rest have been (here you will join me in a sigh) torn up for waste paper. These are but 'scarcely saved.' How just the motto which I have chosen, *Tempus edax rerum*, &c." As it turned out, not all the later Belcher letterbooks suffered this sad fate, for many of them are now in the Massachusetts Historical Society, the last acquisition having been made in 1954.

Apart from his work on the history of New Hampshire, Belknap interested himself in a wide variety of subjects. He stated clearly that he was "always ready to do whatever is in my power to forward any undertaking for the public good." He urged Hazard to prepare a series of memoirs of famous Americans and offered to turn over to him for such a study the materials that he had collected. When Hazard begged off, Bel-

Jeremy Belknap

knap went on with the undertaking himself, finally publishing two volumes entitled *American Biography* (Boston, 1794-98). He called for the establishment of a "Republic of Letters" in America, thinking this a fitting complement to the republican form of government. His intense feelings on this point burst out in the sentence: "I am so far an enthusiast in the cause of America as to wish she may shine Mistress of the Sciences, as well as the Asylum of Liberty." Election to the American Philosophical Society in Philadelphia as an honorary member pleased him, but he accepted only after he made it clear that he would be a working member. He had a part in the establishment of the American Academy of Arts and Sciences in Boston, and here too he proved that he did not take membership in any organization lightly.

A constant stream of communications issued from Belknap's pen on such diverse subjects as natural history, population statistics, and the need for a stronger central government. These eventually found their way into learned society publications or newspapers. His account of his famous walking tour in the White Mountains with six other gentlemen in July, 1784, has often been printed. Belknap, short and corpulent, was the only member of the party not to reach the top of Mount Washington. He later said ruefully: "You will not wonder that such a quantity of matter could not ascend the White Mountains farther than *it* did: 'The spirit was willing, but the flesh (i.e. the lungs) weak.'" The appearance of the first volume of Belknap's *History of New Hampshire* in 1784, heralded by a fine prospectus which he proudly proclaimed because of its "American workmanship," was a source of great satisfaction to him. It was followed by two more volumes in 1791 and 1792. Unfortunately, merit and financial profit do not always go hand in hand. Belknap's solid reputation as a historian is based largely on this work which has been declared "remarkable for its research, impartiality, and literary merit." But it was years before Belknap realized enough from sales to pay the printing bills.

Increasing dissatisfaction with his post in Dover, brought about mainly by disputes over his salary, caused Belknap to resign in September, 1786. For a time, he considered taking the editorship of the *Columbian Magazine* in Philadelphia, but he decided against this move when he received a call on January 30, 1787, to become the minister to the Federal Street Church in Boston. He accepted and was installed on April 4, 1787. Here he remained until his death, happy and contented in the company of congenial associates, continuing his historical researches, and taking an active part in promoting the political and social causes that he thought essential to the betterment of the community and nation. He wanted a strong central government and supported with all his weight the ratification of the Federal Constitution in Massachusetts. He favored a system of national defense, improved inland navigation, home manufactures, public education, and a national religion that would not favor one sect at the expense of another. He was instrumental in securing the passage of an act in Massachusetts (1788) against the slave trade, served on the Harvard Board of Overseers and various philanthropic associations, and was chiefly responsible for founding the Massachusetts Historical Society, an organization that was to be his chief interest during the remaining years of his life.

Just when the idea of a historical society came into Belknap's mind is not known. By September 30, 1787, he was talking of a "collection of dead materials for the use of a future historian" but foresaw difficulties in arousing interest in the scheme. The idea of such a collection was certainly in the minds of many others. John Adams wrote to Belknap about the value of private letters as commentaries on public ones, pointing out that they would be necessary "to shew the secret springs." He urged the preservation of the records of the revolution: "Some of these ought not to be public, but they ought not to be lost. My experi-

Jeremy Belknap

ence has very much diminished my faith in the veracity of History; it has convinced me that many of the most important facts are concealed; some of the most important characters but imperfectly known; many false facts imposed on historians and the world; and many empty characters displayed in great pomp. All this, I am sure, will happen in our American history."

John Pintard, the future founder of the New-York Historical Society, called on Belknap on August 10, 1789, and spoke of his desire to form a society of antiquarians. Paine Wingate (1739-1838), member of Congress, on August 1, 1789, agreed with Belknap that public libraries were proper repositories for such printed papers as the Journals of Congress which in time would become rare. Other Bostonians indicated an interest in Belknap's scheme as the year passed and urged that a beginning be made. On August 27, 1790, Belknap wrote to Hazard: "This morning I have written something, and communicated it to the gentlemen who spoke of it yesterday. How it will issue, time must determine. If it should come to any thing you shall hear farther." The "something" was the "Plan for an Antiquarian Society, August, 1790," a document that has been truly called "a charter of the historical society movement."

This "Plan" called for the establishment of a state historical society and urged other states to organize similar societies that would keep closely in touch with one another through correspondence and by an exchange of publications. Four gentlemen demonstrated an interest in Belknap's plan, and they and Belknap later asked five friends to co-operate with them in the undertaking. All accepted, and eight of these ten original members met on January 24, 1791, to organize what was first called "The Historical Society"—a name changed in 1794 to the "Massachusetts Historical Society." Belknap described the infant society to Hazard in his letter of February 19, 1791: "We have now formed our Society; and it is dubbed, not the Antiquarian, but the 'Historical Society.' It consists at present of only 8, and

Keepers of the Past

is limited to 25. We intend to be an *active*, not a *passive*, literary body; not to lie waiting, like a bed of oysters, for the tide (of communication) to flow in upon us, but to *seek* and *find*, to *preserve* and communicate literary intelligence, especially in the historical way." Actually the membership consisted of ten at the time and a limit of thirty resident members and thirty corresponding members was set.

Jeremy Belknap became the corresponding secretary and was the great force in the society until his death. He helped find quarters for it, gave generously of his own holdings of rare books and manuscripts, and saw to it that a publication, the Massachusetts Historical Society *Collections,* was started that would achieve one of his major aims, the multiplication of copies of rarities. He found time to bring out in book form *The Foresters* (1792), an amusing allegory of the history of the British colonies in North America which had appeared serially in the *Columbian Magazine,* and delivered before the society, at its request, a *Discourse intended to Commemorate the Discovery of America by Christopher Columbus* (1792). On June 9, 1796, he left Boston with Jedidiah Morse (1761-1826), the geographer, on a six-hundred mile trip to and from Oneida, New York, to inspect the mission there at the request of the Board of Commissioners of the society established in Scotland for Propagating Christian Knowledge. News of this journey amused a friend in Scotland who wrote: "Are you as fat as when I knew you? for, to tell the truth, I was disposed to smile at the idea of the good-natured Dr. Belknap sweating in the heats of summer, and smarting under the bite of millions of musquetoes, in a religious progress to the tribe of the cylindrical stone." The journal of this tour is published in the Massachusetts Historical Society *Proceedings.*

But neither "musquetoes" nor heat would have stopped Jeremy Belknap from completing his task. To get the sources of our history was his constant aim, and he would not have allowed personal discomfort to stand in the way. There is a constant

Jeremy Belknap

reminder of this devotion in the rich collections in the Massachusetts Historical Society that came to it under his aegis. His philosophy of collecting was summed up neatly in a letter to Hazard in 1795: "There is nothing like having a *good repository,* and keeping a *good look-out,* not waiting at home for things to fall into the lap, but prowling about like a wolf for prey." This he continued to do until he died of apoplexy on June 20, 1798. It would have gratified him to know that now in his beloved United States there are thousands of collectors in historical agencies whose aim, like his own, is to collect, preserve, and publish the records of our past.

SOURCES

Belknap Papers, in Massachusetts Historical Society *Collections,* 5th Ser., II-III (1877); 6th Ser., IV (1891).
Cole, Charles W. "Jeremy Belknap: Pioneer Nationalist," *New England Quarterly,* X (1937), 743-51.
[Marcou, Jane Belknap]. *Life of Jeremy Belknap.* New York, 1847.
Riley, Stephen T. *The Massachusetts Historical Society, 1791-1959.* Boston, 1959.

John Pintard

by James J. Heslin

For thirteen years after its founding in 1791, the Massachusetts Historical Society was the only such institution in existence. Not until 1804 did the second historical society, The New-York Historical Society, come into being through the efforts of John Pintard, a remarkably public-spirited man.

John Pintard was born in New York City on May 18, 1759, but within a year after his birth, the death of his parents left him orphaned and he was raised and educated by his uncle, Lewis Pintard. After attending school in Hempstead, Long Island, New York, where he distinguished himself as a Latin scholar, Pintard attended the College of New Jersey, now Princeton. In 1776, as he neared graduation, the entire college prepared to enlist against the British; professors became captains, and they enrolled their sudents as soldiers. Although Pintard was too young to enlist he marched along to New York with a company recruited by his professor of mathematics. Shortly afterward, during a lull in the campaign, the company returned to Princeton and Pintard, despite his disobedience, received his degree. After graduation, the young man went to live with his uncle Lewis in New Rochelle, New York, and when Lewis Pintard was appointed by General Washington to act as commissary for

John Pintard

American prisoners in New York City, John was chosen to be his uncle's deputy. It was John Pintard's duty to obtain such articles as might help to alleviate the lot of the prisoners and, so far as possible, make their confinement bearable.

It was not a cheerful task for the young man. Overcrowding and poor sanitation frequently caused illness and death among captive American soldiers imprisoned on board ships in New York harbor or in various buildings throughout the city. So deplorable did the plight of the prisoners become, as a result of crowded quarters, that a number were released in December, 1777, but many of them were physically unable to travel to their homes.

John Pintard performed the duties of his office until 1780 when he was finally released from his post, at which time he went to Paramus, New Jersey. Here he met Miss Elizabeth Brasher, whom he married in 1785, and the couple moved to New York where Pintard went into business for himself at 12 Wall Street as a merchant in trade with the East Indies.

In 1789, the young businessman was elected assistant alderman of the East Ward in New York City, an office to which he was re-elected annually until 1792. In 1790, while still holding this position, he was also elected to the legislature of New York State and served in the legislative session held in New York City from January to March of that year.

These were happy days for the Pintard family. Pintard's business was flourishing and he soon became well known in New York. His handsome appearance and his friendly manner made a favorable impression on friends and strangers alike, and although Pintard was never gifted as a public speaker, his conversation in private was lively and engaging. In March of 1792, however, calamity struck. William Duer, a friend for whom Pintard had endorsed notes in the amount of one million dollars, failed in business. Duer was jailed for debt in March, 1792, and his creditors promptly began to converge on Pintard.

Keepers of the Past

In an effort to satisfy his debt, John Pintard gave up his ships, cargoes, house, furniture—all his property of any value. He moved his family across the Hudson River to Newark, and for eight years, Pintard lived in New Jersey bravely enduring the misfortune that had caused him to lose his possessions and leave the city he loved. While in Newark, he made his livelihood as a member of a commission for erecting bridges over the Hackensack and Passaic rivers. Still another severe blow befell him when Duer's unsatisfied creditors had Pintard jailed for debt. He was arrested and confined to the Newark prison on July 15, 1797, where he remained until August, 1798. Pintard's imprisonment, although disagreeable, was not considered disgraceful, in view of the nature of the debt that caused his confinement. Not until September, 1800, when Pintard took advantage of federal legislation approved that year and declared himself bankrupt, was he able to start anew.

For a short while after he returned to New York, Pintard was a book auctioneer and, later, editor of the *New York Daily Advertiser*. He even visited New Orleans in 1802 with the thought of settling there or even farther west, but he finally abandoned these plans and returned to New York. In 1804, he was appointed clerk to the Corporation of New York and city inspector, and although he never regained his fortune, he gradually assumed his former role in civic and cultural enterprises.

New York in 1804 was a small city with a population of about 75,000, but it showed clearly the signs of growth that were to make it the large metropolis of today. In 1804, there were many men and women who could still remember vividly the British occupation of the city during the revolution and the raising of the American flag when the British evacuated New York. John Pintard himself had acted to rename, in honor of American patriots, streets that formerly bore names associated with British rule, such as Duke, Princess, and King. Pintard's pride in New York and his recollections of the War for Independence made

John Pintard

him more determined than ever to see the establishment of an organization that, hopefully, would preserve the records of the founding of the young American republic.

John Pintard, always interested in history, had observed the progress of the Massachusetts Historical Society with whose founder, the Reverend Jeremy Belknap, he was acquainted. In 1789, while on a visit to Boston, Pintard had met Belknap and, during the course of the meeting, Pintard urged the formation of a "Society of American Antiquarians"—an organization that would collect, preserve, and disseminate the "antiquities" of America. Since Belknap himself, while writing his *History of New Hampshire,* had realized the need for some such institution in which scholars might find useful documentary material, Pintard's suggestion was most welcome. The common interests of the two men ripened into friendship, and they frequently corresponded, so that, in one sense, the first two historical societies in the United States had a common bond.

Pintard's hope for an institution in New York which would concern itself with the preservation of historical materials finally materialized on November 20, 1804. On that day, he and ten other men similarly motivated, met in New York's City Hall and agreed to form themselves into a society that would collect and preserve whatever related to the natural, civil, or ecclesiastical history of the United States in general, and of New York State in particular. At this first meeting, which established The New-York Historical Society, those present also appointed a committee to draw up a draft of a constitution.

John Pintard's strength as an organizer lay in his art of personal persuasion and in his skill in writing appeals to the public. It was said of him that: "He could indite a handbill that would enflame the minds of the people for any good work. He could call a meeting with the pen of a poet, and before the public met, he would have arranged the doings for a perfect success. He knew the weak point of every man, and he would gratify the vanity of men and get their money, and accomplish his good purpose without any of them suspecting that they were merely the respectable names and money tolls that Mr. Pintard required."

It is quite likely that John Pintard either wrote, or strongly influenced, the fledgling society's first appeal to the public which appeared in various newspapers in New York, on February 13, 1805. This appeal from the society stated that its intention was to rescue important documents that might be destroyed or lost through indifference or neglect. Included in this public appeal was the following statement which undoubtedly reflected Pintard's own philosophy: "Without the aid of original records and authentic documents, history will be nothing more than a well-combined series of ingenious conjectures and amusing fables."

The material that The New-York Historical Society was seeking was extensive, including among other things: biographical memoirs; statistical tables of diseases, births, deaths, and population; newspapers, especially those before 1783; magazines; accounts of exports and imports; maps; narratives of voyages and travels; and Indian captivities. To answer any further questions that might arise from the public, a questionnaire of twenty-three items was also printed, listing specific information desired by the Society in relation to early settlers, fortifications, Indian tribes, schools, early purchases of book sellers, laws, and records of territorial disputes. Five hundred copies of this questionnaire were printed in April, 1805, and mailed to various persons in New York.

On January 10, 1809, the society petitioned the legislature for an act of incorporation that was authorized a month later. The institution was formally named "The New-York Historical Society"—and to this day it retains the use of the hyphen.

In the belief that the society's book collection would grow faster if it had a substantial body of useful books as a nucleus,

John Pintard

John Pintard, in 1807, offered to sell his own library at cost to the society. It was obvious to the society that such an acquisition was useful but it took two years to raise the first payment and not until September 15, 1809, was the collection purchased.

The New-York Historical Society was among those affected by the outbreak of the War of 1812. The threat of a British bombardment or invasion of the city, with possible destruction of its building and collections, caused concern to the officers of the society. During the initial uneasiness accompanying the onset of the war, John Pintard engaged himself in a search for a place of safety for the society's holdings.

Meanwhile, housing was but one of the society's problems. There was also the perennial matter of inadequate funds with which to continue its collecting. In May, 1815, New York City sold the Government House in which the society was housed, and it became urgent to find new quarters. Pintard worked manfully helping to pack the society's library and move it to a store on Vesey Street in lower Manhattan. This was hard physical labor for a man of fifty-six, and Pintard described himself as a "perfect galley slave." Fortunately, rooms in the old Alms House, which was then empty and renamed the New York Institution, became available in May, 1816. The following month the society moved into the building.

Pintard was jubilant. The society now had four rooms and storage space in the basement, and all this was free except for "the yearly rent of one peppercorn, if lawfully demanded." Pintard, at this time, wrote to his daughter in New Orleans that he intended to confine all of his attention in the future to The New-York Historical Society, and he permitted himself some expression of joy at the fact that he had taken part in bringing to life and nourishing "this embryo of a very valuable institution and legacy to posterity." On July 9, 1816, the society met formally in its new home for the first time.

On October 12, 1816, in recognition of Pintard's labors, the society voted to commission the artist John Trumbull to paint Pintard's portrait, and this portrait is now one of the Society's chief treasures.

At this time, Pintard held several paying positions. He was secretary of the Mutual Insurance Company, clerk of the Sailor's Snug Harbor, and recording secretary of the American Bible Society. In addition, this indefatigable man held a number of honorary positions, among them secretary of the American Academy of Fine Arts; curator of the Literary and Philosophical Society; trustee of the New York Society Library; treasurer of the Episcopal Theological Seminary Library; vestryman of St. Esprit, the French Huguenot Church; and recording secretary of The New-York Historical Society. Little wonder that he wrote to his daughter on December 4, 1816, saying that he proposed to "resign all my blushing honors" except for his connection with The New-York Historical Society which, he wrote, "I shall cherish to my last day."

The tenancy of the New-York Historical Society in the New York Institution was a time of considerable satisfaction to John Pintard. He was pleased by the growth of the society that was now demonstrating the results of his "struggles almost against hope." In a letter to his daughter on June 27, 1817, Pintard, in his characteristically generous fashion, praised others for their constant support and encouragement. In January, 1818, he again wrote to his daughter, expressing the hope that the society's library might become similar to "the extensive libraries of the Old World inestimably valuable to the erudite scholar."

By 1819, however, intrigues and dissension among the officers of the society caused anguish to Pintard. The fact that newcomers who had had no role in the early development of the society were seeking election to top offices, to the exclusion of the men who had nurtured the institution, angered him. For a time, Pintard considered withdrawing entirely from his cherished institution, and although he did, in fact, resign as recording secretary in 1819, he accepted the post of treasurer which he held through 1827.

"Shameful intrigues," to quote Pintard's phrase, were disturbing enough, but more dangerous to the life of the Society was the now perilous state of its finances. By 1824, the society had a debt of nearly $10,000, and included in this amount was $1,400 owed to Pintard for books he had purchased for the society's library out of his own funds. In desperation, it was proposed that the society sell its library to pay its bills, a suggestion that aroused great protest. On May 4, 1825, the committee charged with settling the society's financial obligations "very reluctantly" placed an advertisement in *The Commercial Advertiser* offering for sale "the choice and rare Library of the Society," an advertisement that the editor of the newspaper felt called upon to state in print had been inserted "with deep mortification."

This turn of events, understandably, was a bitter blow to John Pintard; for over two decades he had labored to build up the society, and it now appeared that his work was in vain. After January, 1825, Pintard no longer appeared at meetings of the society.

In 1827, fortunately, the state of New York came to the society's rescue when the legislature passed a bill appropriating $5,000 for the use of the society. The receipt of this money was contingent, however, upon the society's liquidating its debt of $7,500. The society managed to pay all of its debts except for $1,400 which, ironically, was owed to Pintard for the books he had purchased. Regrettably, Pintard was unable to produce vouchers for the amount owed to him, and he never received any of the money that was his proper due. The library, which still had not been sold, was now safe, but Pintard received no remuneration.

The misfortunes of the society, temporarily alleviated by the appropriation from New York State, resumed their dreary course in May, 1829, when the Common Council of New York ordered the society to vacate by August the rooms it occupied in the New York Institution.

The move from the New York Institution to rented rooms at the corner of Broadway and Chamber Street, in April, 1832, seemed to be a further manifestation of the society's decline. To be sure, valuable gifts of manuscripts, books, and other material continued to be acquired, but the treasury contained only $4.28, and from June, 1833, to January, 1836, the society held no meetings whatever.

But, somehow, the society survived, and in the spring of 1837 moved to Stuyvesant Institute at 659 Broadway. It then inaugurated a series of lectures that were sufficiently successful financially to increase the society's funds. Increased membership, revenue received from lectures, and the hope of moving soon to New York University sustained the morale of the society.

In April, 1841, New York University offered rent-free rooms in its building on Washington Square—in return for which the library of the society was to be open to students of the university, and expenses, other than rent, were to be shared jointly. During the summer of 1841, the society moved into the university's building, and with this move came a new lease on life. Membership increased further, the collections were strengthened, and there was occasion for rejoicing when the society met for the first time in its new rooms on Tuesday evening, October 5, 1841.

It was particularly gratifying that the society's affairs began to prosper in the early 1840's, because John Pintard was now old and sick and had not much longer to live. Time is not always given men to see the results of their labors brought to fruition, but, happily, John Pintard lived to see the society attain the role for which he had worked and planned. Before he died on June 21, 1844, at the age of eighty-five, Pintard had the satisfaction of knowing that the organization he had founded was well on its way to success,

John Pintard

At its regular meeting on October 1, 1844, the society adopted the following resolution in honor of John Pintard, its founder: "Resolved, That in the decease of John Pintard, L.L.D., this Society has lost one of its earliest and most devoted friends, one of those, indeed, to whom the institution owes its origin, and much of its usefulness. Resolved, That the memory of Mr. Pintard is cherished by the members of the Society, for the many excellent features of his private and public character."

SOURCES

Barrett, Walter. *The Old Merchants of New York City*. New York, 1889. Vol. II.
Pintard, John. *Letters from John Pintard*, in The New-York Historical Society *Collections*, 1937, 1938, 1939, 1940.
Vail, R. W. G. *Knickerbocker Birthday*. New York, 1954.

Lyman Copeland Draper

by Larry Gara

In 1853, the Reverend Charles Lord, a founder of the young Wisconsin Historical Society, confided to a friend and co-worker in the cause of history: "I think that Mr. Draper, who is engaged in historical researches, and expects, I believe, to be a resident of Wisconsin, and I suppose of Madison, will be of service to us in our Society."[1]

Lyman Copeland Draper proved, indeed, to be of service to the society and to the people of Wisconsin. It was largely through his efforts that the society was reorganized under a state charter in 1854, and it was under his thirty-seven years of leadership that it became the outstanding institution of its kind in the nation. With only limited financial aid from the state, Draper built from virtually nothing a society that included at the time of his retirement 110,000 volumes, a magnificent collection of manuscripts and newspapers, a museum, and a portrait gallery. With each year's annual report came a revealing statement of new growth in all aspects of the society's activities. All of this brought recognition to Draper and to Wisconsin. In 1871, Cyrus Woodman, a former resident of the state, urged newly-elected Governor C. C. Washburn to put a good word for the Historical Society in his inaugural address. Draper, he

Lyman Copeland Draper

said, "notwithstanding some weaknesses deserves great credit for what he has done to build up that Society. By it the State is known and judged abroad more than by any other single institution, I suppose."[2]

Long before he moved to Wisconsin, Lyman Draper had acquired a national reputation as a historical collector. As a youth in western New York, he had thrilled to the stories told by old settlers and veterans of the Indian wars. Reading historical accounts, begun as a boyhood hobby, became a lifelong habit. From the start of his historical studies, he had noted discrepancies of fact in varying accounts of the same events, and he set about to examine the sources for himself. Going directly to the sources became another Draper habit. In 1833, when only seventeen, he wrote to former President James Madison, requesting a sketch of his life. The same year, dreaming of a career as a historian, he made his debut as an author with a memoir of Charles Carroll of Carrolltown, published in the *Rochester Gem*. As a college student at the Granville Literary and Theological Institution, (later Denison University) in Ohio, Draper continued his historical pursuits, and from time to time, he sent other essays to be published in the Rochester newspaper. Increasingly, his interest in history centered around the incidents of western expansion and settlement. At college, he studied the writings of Judge James Hall, Humphrey Marshall, and others who concentrated on the subject matter of western history. There, too, he became attached to two other causes that profoundly influenced the direction of his life: the Baptist church and the Democratic party. These interests supplemented rather than replaced his passion for history, and he used both Baptist and Democratic connections in ferreting out information and material for his historical labors.

For one so diminutive—only five feet tall and weighing slightly more than a hundred pounds—Lyman Draper was a dynamo of nervous energy. Working steadily for many hours

Keepers of the Past

at a stretch, he accumulated during his lifetime a collection of historical material that in sheer size and value would have been a credit to any library with a large staff of trained workers. Born on September 4, 1815, on a farm near Buffalo, Draper was himself a son of the frontier. The history of the country west of the Alleghenies, mostly from 1756 to 1812, became his major interest. His stated mission was to rescue from oblivion the forgotten heroes of the border wars and early settlements, but first he had to gather the source materials needed to write an accurate account.

He began his collecting by writing to descendants and acquaintances of the pioneer heroes. For one whose thirst for the most minute detail and elusive fact seemed unquenchable, the limitations of correspondence soon became obvious, and early in his career, Draper began carrying a pencil and notebook with him at all times. In October of 1843, he undertook the first of a series of research trips that proved fruitful in the gathering of letters, diaries, and other manuscript materials, as well as recorded interviews. The trip lasted five months and took the energetic historian through parts of Tennessee, Kentucky, and Virginia. On his travels, he collected material from scores of interviews concerning Daniel Boone, George Rogers Clark, James Robertson, John Sevier, and other pioneers. Draper never ceased collecting. In fact, his insistence on getting all of the available facts before committing himself in writing proved a major impediment to his scholarly work. By 1868, he had traveled 46,000 miles in the interest of research and had collected thousands of documents. Yet, at the end of his life, he had published only one book-length monograph, *King's Mountain and Its Heroes*.

Although writer's cramp and other physical afflictions plagued Draper when he set about composing prose, no such difficulty arose when he was patiently filling hundreds of notebooks with the oral reminiscences of people who had known

Lyman Copeland Draper

those pioneers he was determined to rescue from oblivion. The questions he asked were not always those which would most interest a later generation of historians, but to Draper they were important in establishing the facts of history. He wanted to know with certainty which of the pioneer legends were based on facts and which were fictitious. He devoted many hours to establishing such details as the authenticity of Samuel Brady's famous leap across the Cuyahoga River and the specific places where Daniel Boone had carved his intitials on the bark of trees. Francis Parkman and some other scholars warned Draper about relying too much on the memories of old men and he himself was aware of the danger. When possible he compared accounts of various persons, and even while he was listening attentively and rapidly recording the inverviews, he sometimes added in the margin comments indicating that a particular informant's version of events must be taken with "many grains of allowance."[3]

In 1853, Lyman Draper moved to Wisconsin at the invitation of an old college chum, Charles A. Larrabee, who was active in Democratic politics and interested in establishing the new historical society on a firm footing. The society had already had several unsuccessful starts before Draper arrived. The newcomer made friends with those who had prepared the groundwork for a going society, and before long, he became a leader of the group. He and Larrabee drafted a charter that, when approved by the legislature, established the State Historical Society of Wisconsin, whose object was "to collect, embody, arrange, and preserve in authentic form a library of books, pamphlets, maps, charts, manuscripts, papers, paintings, statuary and other materials illustrative of the history of the State," as well as "to secure from oblivion the memory of its early pioneers, and to obtain and preserve narratives of their exploits, perils, and hardy adventures." The society could also "exhibit faithfully the antiquities and the past and present condition and resources of

Wisconsin," promote historical study by lectures, and "diffuse and publish information relating to the description and history of the State."[4]

For a year, Draper served the society as corresponding secretary without salary, and he devoted the remaining years of his life to its service. In his new position, he proved capable of getting regular support from a reluctant legislature and made the residents of Wisconsin aware of their rich heritage of history. Draper rejected the idea of an aristocratic society with a highly select membership and only perfunctory occasional meetings, which some earlier promoters had favored, and built instead an organization that would provide exceptionally good library resources for scholars in Wisconsin and elsewhere. He broadened the base of the society's support with numerous honorary and corresponding memberships, but it was left to a later administration to build from Draper's foundation a truly democratic society serving all the people of the state.

Draper was a born promoter. His energetic and enthusiastic manner proved contagious, and he attracted people's attention to the causes he espoused. He immediately became an ardent booster of Madison, where he located, and described in glowing terms and thorough detail its resources and prospects in a forty-eight page pamphlet entitled *Madison, the Capital of Wisconsin: Its Growth, Progress, Condition, Wants and Capabilities*. Madison's city council printed and distributed ten thousand copies, and the brochure was reprinted in *The Wisconsin State Directory* for 1857 and 1858.

In Wisconsin, Draper also continued his private historical collecting and vast correspondence and called the attention of many outside the state to the historical society. Men of wealth and influence in Wisconsin and beyond the state received honorary memberships and an invitation to contribute books, manuscripts, newspaper files, and other needed items to the society's collections. Early Wisconsin residents were asked for portraits to be added to the growing portrait gallery. A list of "Objects of Collection Desired by the Society" included such items as personal narratives, newspapers, college catalogs, drawings of Indian mounds, and coins. And all phases of the collection grew annually. By 1876, the society could boast a library of 65,000 titles. When Draper took charge eighteen years earlier, the entire library of fifty volumes had been comfortably housed in a single small cabinet.

After more than a decade in the basement of the Baptist Church, the society's objects were moved, in 1866, to the second floor of the south wing of the newly completed state capitol building. Eighteen years later, it was provided still more space in the same building. Draper's dream of a separate, fireproof building to house the society's collection did not materialize until nine years after his death.

Although Draper concentrated on the facts of early western history, he displayed, at times, a remarkably broad view concerning the past. He advised Wisconsin residents not only to treasure the achievements of the pioneers but also to gather and preserve the records of those "adventurous companies who planned and executed the noble improvements" in the state, as well as the documents concerning the "religious, literary and humanitarian institutions" and economic life. When urging Wisconsin to establish a tax-supported system of school libraries, Draper listed representative men and events that he believed should be mentioned in the books. Political and military leaders and events were only a few of those in his compilation. School libraries should include works that would tell "in a truthful, captivating manner," the stories of the "heroes of ancient times," the crusades and the revival of learning, Columbus, Galileo, Newton, and Franklin, the early settlers in the American colonies, and such significant inventors as Richard Arkwright, James Watt, Eli Whitney, Robert Fulton, and Samuel F. B. Morse.[5]

Keepers of the Past

His single term as Wisconsin's superintendent of public instruction, from 1858 to 1860, was the only period in which Draper held an elective political office. As superintendent, he made a careful study of Wisconsin's schools in comparison with similar institutions in other states. His painstaking care and scholarly methods contributed to the very ambitious and complete school report for 1858. The nearly four-hundred-page book was the most detailed report of any Wisconsin governmental agency. The whole volume, with its statistical survey, argued for more and improved schools through better teacher training, graded schools, a township rather than a district school system, and school libraries. Even though Wisconsin voters turned down Draper's bid for a second term as school superintendent, he was able to contemplate his service to education with justifiable satisfaction. He left the office with the school picture brighter than he had found it, and he had succeeded, by dint of incessant work, in getting the legislature to support his project for school libraries. Yet history remained his primary concern and as an anonymous correspondent put it, there was "lots of timber" for school superintendents "but historical investigators are rare." Draper's office-holding made him "guilty of polygamy" in his interests. "Rely upon it, my friend," he advised, "polygamy won't do, when you wish to beget great offspring."[6]

Even while he was state superintendent of public instruction, Draper found ample time to devote to his historical pursuits as well as to the affairs of the society. When he undertook to build up the State Historical Society of Wisconsin, he determined that it would soon become "the best Historical Library in the North West extant" and his boast was by no means an empty one. Everything, including the affairs of his immediate family—a wife and adopted daughter—was subordinated to his historical interests and the single-mindedness produced results. By 1875, he could proudly tell the society's members: "Our library is doing a silent, noble, effective work...accumulating and disseminating as it does wisdom and knowledge to all classes of society."[7] Several other historical societies looked to Wisconsin as the model to emulate. Historical societies in Minnesota, Iowa, and Kansas followed closely along Wisconsin's pattern, and when after the Civil War southern societies began to revive their activities, a number of them yearned for the kind of persistent, dedicated leadership that Draper had provided Wisconsin. The Chicago *Tribune,* in a feature story about Draper, stated that he was "a Historical Society in himself."[8]

Part of Draper's responsibilities involved writing. The magic power of a deadline seemed to stimulate Draper's pen into a productive course. Each year he prepared an annual report that proudly listed new acquisitions, improvements, and general growth of the society. He also edited the ten volumes of *Wisconsin Historical Collections* which appeared during his tenure as secretary. The *Collections* were a model of how to edit and publish reminiscences and other sources covering a wide range of historical material. Editing proved more compatible with Draper's temperament than more extended historical composition. He enjoyed adding details and bits of interesting information in footnotes to the works he published. However, he also contributed some original articles. During his last year with the society, he wrote an essay on the "Autographs of Signers of the Declaration of Independence, and of the Constitution" which appeared in the tenth volume of *Collections* and immediately brought recognition to the author as the nation's leading authority on the subject.

Draper's driving ambition to write a series of definitive books on western history was never fulfilled, but his collecting and his plans for writing seemed to satisfy his craving for accomplishment. It was the gathering and sorting of materials that intrigued him, though he never consciously abandoned his proposed series of volumes. In 1846, he issued a two-page printed circular that called attention to his achievement in collecting five thousand manuscripts and five thousand pages of notes, and he announced his intention to begin work on a series of "Sketches of the Lives of the Pioneers." A new distraction in the form of a lead to some important George Rogers Clark papers provided the first of numerous delays. From time to time, he actually began writing several of his proposed books, including biographies of Daniel Boone and George Rogers Clark, which he believed would be his most significant scholarly contribution. He wrote a dozen chapters of the Boone book before setting it aside for other matters, and he almost completed a critical study of the 1775 Mecklenburg Declaration of Independence which he concluded was spurious. At various times, he tried to work with co-authors, but three such literary partnerships proved to be fruitless.

In fact, two of Draper's partnerships ended with considerable bad feeling. He was possessed of a very strong will and found it difficult to work closely with others. A number of personal idiosyncrasies also affected aspects of his life. He was plagued by various physical ailments and he frequently relied upon unusual and unorthodox treatment, at times even getting his entire medical advice and prescriptions by correspondence from doctors who had never examined him. When Orson Fowler, a phrenologist, visited Madison, Draper was among those who sought advice from him. In later years, he even dropped his interest in the Baptist church and became a devoted spiritualist. He called upon the spirits not only for medical advice but for historical information as well, though he never added any of the "spirit" material to his regular collection of documents.

It was his collection that attracted the attention of other historians, who often wrote Draper for assistance with their own research problems. Especially in his younger days, Draper was unusually generous in providing other writers with some of his own source material. Francis Parkman, Jared Sparks, Brantz Mayer, A. Randall, and the Reverend James H. Perkins, the latter two from the Cincinnati Historical Society, were among the many who received material from Draper. Perkins, like Draper, was exact in his methods and appreciative of the help he received. "If all our inquirers into Wn History were as manly and generous as you are," he said, "we should make rapid progress."[9]

Yet as time went on, Draper became more crotchety in his habits and more possessive about his collection. Sometimes a request for information reminded him of his own earlier intention of writing on a similar subject and set him momentarily at work on an outline. He did continue to honor requests from older acquaintances and especially favored historical amateurs and antiquarians of Americana. He had little understanding of the newer academic historians who increasingly turned to him for assistance. Edward Channing and Stephen B. Weeks were among those whose requests Draper turned down.

Draper had, after all, acquired his magnificent collection by hard work and personal expense. Many of the items had been purchased outright. Frequent misunderstandings concerning the terms of his ownership plagued him, yet no one could prove that any part of his collection had been acquired fraudulently. He was scrupulous in carefully preserving all the documents that came his way. When he received a bundle of documents that had been rescued from the burning Louisiana statehouse by a Union soldier from Wisconsin, Draper took pains to sort and press them and have them bound into volumes. Then, when the Louisiana Historical Society was reorganized after the war, he sent the documents to the president of the society.

As time went on, Draper came to realize that his real function in life was the collecting and preservation of the raw material of history through the State Historical Society of Wisconsin. Indeed, it was difficult to make a distinction between Draper's private collecting and his work for the society. And as the society expanded its collections and field of activity, the work involved proved too much for a single individual. As early as 1857, Draper had hired Daniel Durrie as society librarian. Durrie also served the society for many years, quietly and ably supplementing the efforts of its energetic corresponding secretary. By the time he reached the age of sixty-nine, Draper had decided to prepare a young man to take over the direction of the society. He chose a journalist-historian, Reuben Gold Thwaites, who, after a period of apprenticeship, became the corresponding secretary in 1887 when Draper technically retired from the position. Many years earlier Cyrus Woodman had told Draper: "When you are gone the Historical Society of Wisconsin will be your monument, more enduring than brass or marble."[10] When the long-time corresponding secretary proved his adeptness as an administrator by preparing to place the society's future affairs in good hands, he could contemplate with pride his many achievements.

Draper had also gained renown during his own lifetime, partly through his own promotional efforts and partly through the work of others. As early as 1851, the Granville Literary and Theological Institution had granted him recognition with an honorary M.A. degree, and years later the University of Wisconsin added an LL.D. to his name. When his name was mentioned to the Granville board of trustees and one of the members asked who Draper was, a professor promptly answered that he was the "Plutarch of Western Hisory." The title was associated with Draper for the rest of his life and was used by William A. Croffut and Reuben Gold Thwaites in their sketches of the historical collector. Both had been associated with Draper and both recounted the story of his single-handed creation of a great personal library and a significant historical society. In 1875, Croffut described Draper as a "small, wiry man, and while his head and beard is silvery, his eyes preserve the brightness and his step the elasticity of youth." Croffut noted the "odd fact" that Draper had published virtually nothing, that he was "naturally a gleaner rather than a compiler," but promised two books would soon be forthcoming. Thwaites' sketch appeared a dozen years later but told virtually the same story: the heroic deeds of Draper's life as a collector-historian. Thwaites placed special emphasis on his mentor's shyness and modesty, traits that hardly described Draper who, for example, had personally given wide circulation, both in the newspapers and in private correspondence, to Croffut's sketch when it appeared.[11]

Lyman Draper died in Madison on August 27, 1891. By the terms of the will, his entire collection went to the society to which he had devoted the best years of his life. After final sorting and arranging, the Draper manuscripts included a total of 478 bound volumes. The acquisition made the State Historical Society of Wisconsin one of the nation's outstanding research centers for western history.

Draper's work exerted a profound influence on the direction of American historical scholarship. His emphasis on the importance of the West was later echoed by many others. His work with western materials had helped to prepare the intellectual environment in which Frederick Jackson Turner wrote and formulated his famous frontier thesis of American history. Countless other scholars mined the rich ores of source material that Draper had accumulated. It was for others to produce the biographies of Daniel Boone, George Rogers Clark, Simon Kenton, Thomas Sumter, and James Harrod, and the studies of border warfare and pioneer settlement that Draper had planned. Indirectly, and at long last, he had accomplished his mission. The books that later scholars produced from Draper's manuscripts rescued from oblivion many of his heroes whose deeds would be virtually unknown without his life work as a collector and promoter of history.

Keepers of the Past

SOURCES AND NOTES

The Draper Papers are in the library of the State Historical Society of Wisconsin, along with those of many of his colleagues and contemporaries in his adopted state. Any study of Lyman C. Draper must necessarily draw heavily upon the late William B. Hesseltine's excellent biography: *Pioneer's Mission: The Story of Lyman Copeland Draper* (Madison, Wis., 1954).

1. The Reverend Charles Lord to Increase A. Lapham, Jan. 3, 1853, in the Lapham Papers. All manuscripts cited are in the State Historical Society of Wisconsin.
2. Cyrus Woodman to C. C. Washburn, Nov. 12, 1871, in the Cyrus Woodman Papers.
3. Notes from interview with Alexander McCollom in the Draper MSS, 31S297.
4. *Wisconsin Historical Collections*, l:xlix-l.
5. "Sixteenth Annual Report of the State Historical Society of Wisconsin," in *Wisconsin Historical Collections*, 6:32-34; *Tenth Annual Report on the Condition and Improvement of the Common Schools and Educational Interests of the State of Wisconsin, For the Year 1858* (Madison, Wis., 1858), 48-49.
6. Unsigned letter from Courtland Village, New York, Dec. 17, 1857, in the Draper Correspondence.
7. Draper to Lapham, Feb. 24, 1854, in the Lapham Papers; *Wisconsin Historical Collections*, 7:70-76.
8. Newport *Wisconsin Mirror*, April 29, 1856, p. 3, col. 2, quoting the Chicago *Tribune*.
9. James H. Perkins to Draper, Feb. 17, 1848, in the Draper MSS, 2Q59.
10. Cyrus Woodman to Draper, Jan. 8, 1869, in the Woodman Papers.
11. Clipping from the *Cincinnati Enquirer*, Oct. 20, 1875, in the Draper Correspondence, dated Dec. 6, 1875; Thwaite's essay on "The Plutarch of Western History" appeared in the January, 1887, issue of the *Magazine of Western History*.

Reuben Gold Thwaites

by Clifford L. Lord

On Saturday, October 18, 1913, Reuben Gold Thwaites, dynamic and popular superintendent of the State Historical Society of Wisconsin, closed his desk and prepared to go home. The annual meeting was five days off but everything was already in order for the event.

Thwaites could reflect with considerable satisfaction on the current situation of the society. Twenty-six years earlier he had succeeded Lyman Copeland Draper as secretary. In the intervening years, the library had more than trebled in size, the collecting of manuscripts had been systematized, and attention had been directed for the first time to both Wisconsin manuscripts and Wisconsin newspapers—to the latter with the help of the Wisconsin Press Association. The legislature had made the society the official depository of the state archives, and important state records had flowed to the society until space ran out. The museum had been transformed from a cabinet of curiosities into a modern instrument of public education, and people from school age to late adulthood had been encouraged by a variety of ploys to visit it frequently. He had even experimented with sending special exhibitions to schools throughout the state and to national expositions. He had reissued the first ten volumes of the society's

Collections and had edited an additional ten volumes himself. To observe the fiftieth anniversary of the Civil War, he had persuaded the legislature to establish a War History Commission—of which he had become secretary—in order to publish a series of works, both primary and secondary, on Wisconsin in the war. The society had acquired its first historic site and had begun the agitation for the restoration of the Territorial Capitol, which would bear fruit eleven years later. He had encouraged and helped establish the first local historical societies as auxiliaries of the state society and had seen them begin preserving important sites, erecting markers, gathering local records and reminiscences, and developing local historical museums.

Wisconsin was, as never before, interested in its history and working at it. As he had foreseen, the legislature had responded to that interest and, beginning in 1907, had increased the state appropriations handsomely. Now the annual appropriation stood at $36,000, where it had been but $8,000 when he took office.[1] Private donors had also responded to the broad appeal of the activities he had successfully initiated, and private fund income had risen during his tenure from $904.61 to $7,152.98 a year.[2]

He had focused attention for the first time on the many ethnic groups in the state, had secured their co-operation in varying degrees for a data-gathering survey, and had been rewarded with several articles and one book-length manuscript on individual groups. He had persuaded the Sons of the American Revolution to finance the publication of three volumes of Draper manuscripts. He had helped the Federation of Women's Clubs set up study programs on Wisconsin history and launch a substantial marker program. He had captured the wholehearted co-operation of the state Archeological Society by naming its key officer, Charles E. Brown, director of the Historical Society's museum. Another large group of markers had resulted. The influence of the society was felt as never before across the state.

Above all there was that handsome building in which he was

Reuben Gold Thwaites

sitting, then the finest historical society and one of the finest library facilities in the country. Careful and intricate maneuvers had brought the society's fine library, then many times the size of that of the university, to the university campus in 1900. The deal had been elaborate, with society and university making a joint approach to the legislature to secure for the society, on land that the university turned back to the state for the purpose, a building that would be jointly occupied until the university could secure its own library building. Just three and a half years after the society moved into its fine new State Street quarters, the wing it had previously occupied in the old Capitol was gutted by fire. By such a narrow chronological margin had the collections, the priceless library, the Draper manuscripts been spared certain destruction. Luck had been with the society on that occasion and frequently during the past quarter century. Things had gone particularly well in the last fifteen years; it was Thwaites who had made them go that way.

He was only sixty, but recognition had already come in many forms. One of the outstanding historical editors of his generation, he had seen 170 volumes to press. To the 73 volumes of the *Jesuit Relations* and the 32 volumes of the *Early Western Travels,* he had added the 8 volumes of the *Original Journals of the Lewis and Clark Expedition,* 26 volumes of society *Proceedings,* 10 volumes of society *Collections,* 10 volumes of the War History Commission, and 12 other titles.[3] In addition, he had written 15 books, including the semi-centennial history of the University of Wisconsin and volumes for the American Nation Series, the Epochs of American History, and (with Louise Phelps Kellogg) the American Commonwealth Series. Two professions had given him their highest honors. He had been president of the American Library Association, a member of its council, a life member of the honorific American Library Institute. Though he had opposed (as unnecessary) the organization of the Mississippi Valley Historical Association, he had been elected one of its early (1912-13) presidents. He had been active in several major projects of the American Historical Association, particularly the European transcripts program and the Conference of Historical Societies, of which he was the real founder and which later became the American Association for State and Local History. He had received a well-earned LL.D. from the University of Wisconsin, and—presumably a mark of self-satisfaction—had begun his autobiography.

He locked the office door, turned into the west corridor of the second floor, down the handsome marble stairway, out the door to State Street. It was for the last time. The following evening he fell ill. Three days later, October 22, 1913, he died.

A memorial service was held December 19 in the new state capitol. The assembly chamber was crowded. Governor Francis E. McGovern was in the chair. Members of the Supreme Court, the University Board of Regents, the Society Board of Curators, staff, faculty, and friends filled the seats and the galleries. The main speaker was Thwaites' close—perhaps closest—friend, Frederick Jackson Turner, returned from Harvard to pay heartfelt tribute to his old colleague. Turner, with a perception almost unique among their colleagues and friends, identified Thwaites' great contribution: "Thwaites was," he said, "the builder of a new type of state historical society."[4] A year before he had written to Frederic Paxson, "To a degree that can hardly yet be recognized, he (Thwaites) has changed the conception of the western (historical) society."[5] Herein lies Reuben Gold Thwaites' prime claim to fame.

What was this new conception? Very simply that the historical society, like the public library, the museum, the art gallery, is an instrument of public education; that service to scholarship alone—important and valuable as it was and is, and basic as it was and is to the purposes of the society—is not enough; the modern society should encourage the amateur and acquaint the broadest possible sector of the public with the values of local history and heritage. This, to Thwaites, was a necessary—not an extraneous or luxurious—function of the historical society in a democracy becoming ever more democratic.

The Society that Thwaites took over from Lyman Copeland Draper in 1887 was—like all historical societies in this country since the Reverend Jeremy Belknap called together a group of his friends to launch the Massachusetts Historical Society—fundamentally a gentleman's club. Its program, like that of Massachusetts before it, involved not only gathering materials for the library and the cabinet of curiosities but the preparation of papers and the editing and publishing of collections of documents and papers to better communicate knowledge to others. A candidate for membership had to be formally proposed and, at least theoretically, could be blackballed. Membership was small and largely restricted in practice to Madison and its immediate environs. Dues were nominal and often were not collected. It was another example of government by crony, so often seen in nineteenth-century America—in churches, hospitals, pre-Carnegie libraries, school boards, even town government, and emphatically in the other gentlemen's clubs of the day.

This was the accepted and usually acceptable pattern of many operations in what was still a substantially stratified society. The America of the second half of the nineteenth century was full of opportunity, on frontier and seaboard alike. Compared to western Europe, democracy was far advanced. But egalitarianism was far more typical of the frontier than of the seaboard, where society was by no means as classless as it was later to become. The present-day historical society has a worrisomely limited appeal to the technician and the worker. A century ago it had none, and very little for any but a small cultured and social elite.

But with the turn of the century came one of the six great periods of democratic advancement in this nation: the Progressive Era. Highest among its hallmarks was a burgeoning faith in the perfectibility of mankind through education. High school attendance jumped precipitately. College attendance rose. The public library, aided by the Carnegie benefactions, assumed new importance in informal public education. The Chautauqua idea was widely accepted and utilized. The Social Gospel came to the fore.

The burgeoning economy, buttressed by the nearly completed network of railroads, the huge supply of cheap labor flooding into the country from abroad, the proliferation of capital and the rise of the large corporation; the greater democracy of the initiative, referendum, recall, and short ballot; the growing effectiveness of craft unions; the rising protests against the unfair use of economic and political power, against trusts and malefactors of great wealth, against political manipulation and the boss—all made this period, despite its manifest contradictions and its opposing stresses, one of great progress for the little man, roughly comparable to the periods of the New Deal and the Great Society.

Progressivism was particularly potent in Wisconsin. As Robert LaFollette, Sr., called the resources of the state university into the service of the state government, University President Charles Van Hise was proclaiming the boundaries of the campus to be the borders of the state, reviving extension services, introducing correspondence study. Politically, Progressivism under LaFollette, Davidson, and McGovern brought the direct primary, a stiff corrupt practices act, civil service, vocational education, the effective regulation of railroads and utilities, minimum wages for women, safety laws, and workmen's compensation.

This was the heady atmosphere in which Thwaites operated. He was a creature of Progressivism and, particularly but not exclusively in Wisconsin, one of the shapers of the educational segment of its development. The great interest of this editor of historical documents, this head of a great research library, came to be the education of the "masses," the educationally underprivileged.

One key agency of public education was the public library. Thwaites became an active organizer of the citizen's committees that were essential to qualify towns for Carnegie library grants, and frequently he was the main speaker at the dedication of the resulting buildings. He was a founder and lifetime member of the Wisconsin Free Library Commission, which brought new standards and new services—and later state aid—to Wisconsin libraries. A great believer in the interchange of ideas through meetings of like-minded people beset with similar problems, he was a founder and one-time president of the Wisconsin Library Association.

An equally important agency in public education in Thwaites's eyes, as in the progressive historical society today, was the museum. No longer a mere cabinet of curiosities, under the theories effectively advocated in the 1890's by G. Brown Goode of the Smithsonian, its exhibits should tell the story of foreign lands and peoples, of natural phenomena, of the flora and fauna of an area, or of local history. Such exhibits unquestionably were of a lower intellectual order, Thwaites acknowledged, than the reference book in the library, but he saw the museum showcase as more attractive and conceivably more stimulating to the common man. As early as 1891, he was talking of the "excellent missionary work" the museum could do among the "masses."[6]

When he finally secured the funds to modernize the museum at Madison, he not only saw to it that the exhibits were reorganized to educate but that all possible means of attracting adults and school groups to the museum were utilized. Convention delegates and wives were sought; school attendance was solicited by mail and personal lecture. Philatelists were given special attention. The Madison Art Association was encouraged to hold its exhibitions in the society galleries. Exhibits were frequently changed. Special exhibits—as many as twenty a year

—were timed for special anniversaries or the visits to Madison of special groups. Then-modern exhibit techniques were introduced. Circulating exhibits to the schools were initiated. Annual attendance—with travel a bit more difficult than today—soon reached the 100,000 mark. He also encouraged the local historical societies, which he was bringing into being in Wisconsin, to start their own museums, using space in the local library or courthouse, if possible, until they could afford their own buildings.

These local societies, for which there were many eastern precedents, especially in New England, he saw as a means of enlisting more people in the important work of collecting manuscripts, securing reminiscences, writing and publishing local history, as well as creating their own local museums. He actively sponsored their establishment in Wisconsin as arms or auxiliaries (unlike New England) of the state society, beginning in Green Bay and Ripon. The legislature authorized their incorporation and the expenditure of municipal tax monies for local museums. Bulletins of information were published for their guidance and Thwaites cheerfully traveled the state—or sent staff representatives—to attend their meetings.

He early became interested in historic sites and markers. In the latter, originating in New England during the centennial of independence and in California shortly thereafter, he saw another vehicle of public education, a way of spreading and perpetuating knowledge about the places where history had happened. Not only did he encourage the state and local societies to erect markers, but he stimulated the establishment of the Landmarks Committee of the Federation of Women's Clubs to undertake an extensive program in this field. He persuaded the Wisconsin Archeological Society to mark archeological sites, while encouraging its survey, mapping, excavating and publishing activities.

Markers were inexpensive. The preservation and restoration of sites and historic buildings presented problems of a different financial magnitude. Such tasks could not be undertaken until the affluence of the economy made possible, through either private or public sources, the substantial expenditures involved. Wisconsin was still short of that stage of wealth and interest, yet beginnings were made. Thwaites was well aware that sites and buildings were of far greater educational potential than markers. Not even the historical museum could so effectively re-create the aura of times and events long past. Beginning in the mid-nineteenth century, the east—specifically New York State with the Hasbrouck House (1837), Tennessee with the Hermitage (1856), and private enthusiasts and philanthropists at Mt. Vernon (1860)—had led the way in saving American historic sites for posterity. Under Thwaites, the Wisconsin society acquired its first historic site, that of the blockhouse of a militia fort of the Black Hawk War, with a magnificent view commanding the countryside from Madison on the east to the Sinsinawa Mounds on the west, half the width of the state. It launched, with the Federation of Women's Clubs, a campaign for the preservation of the Territorial Capitol and saw the first local society preserve and restore the oldest house in the state, a pre-Revolutionary wattle structure at Green Bay. A second society preserved the schoolhouse in which Alvin Bovay denominated the Republican party at Ripon, and still another preserved a large Indian mound.

Naturally, with his interest in public education, Thwaites sought to work closely with the schools. He saw local history offering the school teacher a laboratory in the social studies, with source materials immediately at hand. For the semi-centennial of statehood in 1898, which was cut short by the outbreak of the Spanish-American War, he hoped for the widespread participation of the schools in essay contests, exhibits, and collecting programs. The legislature established a special commission, headed by the superintendent of public instruction, and the school children had completed more work than the adult segment of the population when the war practically ended the observance.

He actively sought to enlist others in various educational programs where history was concerned. The revival of university extension, the establishment by the Free Library Commission of a state-wide circulating system of books and pamphlets, and Thwaites's good relations with the Federation of Women's Clubs led quite naturally to the establishment of a study program within the federation. Materials and a study outline prepared by Louise Phelps Kellogg (research associate of the society and first, and to date only, woman president of the Mississippi Valley Historical Association) were supplied by the society to the Free Library Commission to circulate to the women's groups throughout the state.

Pageants, adapted to American use, popularized by Laredo Taft, and soon to be brought to new levels of practicability in Wisconsin by Ethel Rockwell, and other observances of historical anniversaries were further means of attracting substantial public interest, of stimulating and educating the "masses," and of enlisting in a local historical activity people without previous competence in the field, who perhaps would develop a lasting interest in local history. Thwaites traveled the state to encourage such observances.

Thwaites came to seek a large general membership that was representative of a cross-section of the population, not for mere numbers but in order to reach regularly and intimately the largest possible number of those interested in history, to have them ready to stand and be counted, ready to support the good work. He also sought a governing board responsive to public interest but dedicated, as trustees of such an institution must be, to history and its highest standards. With the people of Wisconsin vigorously expressing their independence of political machines and their right to participate in decision-making at all levels of government during the LaFollette period, with travel becoming easier though by no means easy, and with the society largely dependent upon the legislature for its sustenance, it was natural that Thwaites should forsake his predecessor's lack of interest in members outside Madison. He sought a state-wide membership, soon had more members in Milwaukee than Madison. Instead of a board of key members who were residents of Madison, he secured a board with strong state-wide representation and key members well distributed geographically. And he experimented with notable success in holding the annual meeting in various cities around the state.

Thwaites was convinced that with widespread citizen interest and participation in its program of public education, gifts in cash and kind would flow as never before to the society's collections and coffers. This certainly proved to be the case. The legislature took its time—ten years. But beginning in 1907, it began to respond handsomely to his requests, knowing, as it did, the increasing number of people back home in each legislative district interested in, and working in behalf of, the society or its many related activities. The annual appropriation rose rapidly. A museum director was provided for the first time, and a sorely needed addition to the building was authorized in 1911. The collections grew at an unprecedented pace, both in library and museum, and benefactions became numerous. All but one of the society's major bequests were made during Thwaites's administration, though the income of the largest did not become available until some years after his death. Proverbially, nothing succeeds like success. No one ever proved this better in the historical society field than Thwaites.

In behalf of his concepts, Thwaites traveled not only Wisconsin but the country with something of the "missionary zeal" he demanded of his staff. Quite literally from Maine to California, he preached the values of the public library, the museum, public education, and local history to audiences that sought his well-known platform skill. In convention after convention of his peers, among librarians and historians alike, he worked to spread his ideas. And spread they did. His contemporaries in historical societies watched the publications of the Wisconsin Society for new departures; they sought him out at conventions to pick his brain and to tap his latest enthusiasms. Especially through the meetings of the Conference of Historical Societies did he reach his peers, particularly those of the midwestern societies, where his practices and concepts took quick root.

As early as 1900, Thwaites could rightly boast, "This Society (has) moved away from its traditional moorings as an exclusive, almost an aristocratic retreat for the learned alone, and carried on its work of self-popularization.... More and more is the Society commending itself as a practical assistant to intellectual activity among all classes."[7] At that point, he had not yet entered the field of historic sites, study programs, school exhibitions, or pageants and had barely started on markers and local societies. His museum program existed on paper only.

When he died thirteen years later, the distance the Wisconsin society had traveled from its traditional moorings was infinitely greater. He had by then evolved something new in historical societies, something that had already achieved considerable influence in the Midwest, and something that since his death has spread across the country until today hardly a society exists that in some degree has not felt and been influenced by his often anonymous impact.

Thwaites's ideal did not quite match that of the "compleate" modern society. The emancipation of women had not yet advanced sufficiently to bring them into anything like the position they occupy today in the modern historical society. The automobile—which proved not to be the incentive towards socialism which Woodrow Wilson had feared—was in its infancy, and the mobility so essential to the modern development of the historic site and the historical celebration was not yet with us. The use of radio, television, and the self-contained mobile exhibit as vehicles of public education still lay in the future. So did the marked increase in human longevity that has influenced the modern development of the historical society as it has influenced all western society. But the Thwaites concept was remarkably close to the late twentieth-century ideal of the progressive historical society.

What manner of man was this dynamo who in twenty-six years accomplished such wonders and wrought such revolutionary changes in his chosen field of work? The son of English immigrants, he spent his teens on the family farm near Omro, Wisconsin. There he did his chores and attended the public schools. Like most of his contemporaries, he did not go to college though some years later he did take a few graduate courses at Yale, where he became interested in journalism. There he became a member of the fourth estate, a career he was to continue upon his return to Wisconsin with the Oshkosh *Northwestern* and then with the Madison *Wisconsin State Journal,* where he was city editor when Draper chose him at the age of thirty-two to be his assistant and successor.

A short (5'6"), slightly rotund man, he coupled a genial and cordial exterior and a well-remembered skill as a raconteur with an iron will that drove him to prodigious effort and accomplishment and that peremptorily brought to heel those who outraged his sensibilities or fell short of his expectations. Staff members in whom he was disappointed, or outsiders who tried to hoodwink him or capitalize on the society's high reputation, quickly felt the lash of his tongue or pen. At all other times, he was a cheery man. A ready smile, the sometimes twinkling, sometimes flashing brown eyes behind the rimless glasses, the rumpled hair, the easy speech—some of it acquired at the city desk—were characteristics that made him easy to meet. A man of great charm, he made close friends readily. A man of infectious enthusiasm, he won others effectively to his causes. A man interested in getting things done, he readily adapted business methods and devices, even assembly line techniques, to his work.

He never quite lost the slight accent acquired in part from his parents and in part from his early years in Massachusetts. He never—and this was surprising—felt quite at home with the legislators. But he died the best-known man in Wisconsin outside of politics. And he died having set the standards for his field for generations yet unborn.

SOURCES AND NOTES

This essay is based largely on the author's 1963 Burton Lecture of the Historical Society of Michigan which was published separately by the society under the title "Reuben Gold Thwaites and the Progressive Historical Society." It is republished here—with some changes—by permission of the Historical Society of Michigan. It is based largely on the Thwaites Papers and the official archives of the State Historical Society of Wisconsin at Madison, Wisconsin.

1. State Historical Society of Wisconsin, *Proceedings,* 1887, p. 7; *Proceedings,* 1913, p. 23.

2. *Ibid.,* 1887, p. 10; 1913, pp. 52-54.

3. For bibliography of Thwaites' writings, see F. J. Turner: *Reuben Gold Thwaites: A Memorial Address* (Madison, Wis., 1914), pp. 63-94. To these totals should be added at least eighty-one published addresses, articles, pamphlets and reports, seventy SHSW *Bulletins of Information* and seven SHSW *Handbooks.*

4. Turner, *Reuben Gold Thwaites,* p. 58.

5. Turner to Paxson, Feb. 19, 1912, in State Historical Society Archives 27/1/3, Administration, Genl. Correspondence, 1914-1930, Box 70.

6. State Historical Society of Wisconsin, *Proceedings,* 1891, p. 66.

7. *Ibid.,* 1899, p. 9.

Dixon Ryan Fox

by John Allen Krout

In the pageant of the arts and sciences the local historian does not figure brightly. He is tolerated only as a poor relation of the mighty scholars who chronicle the deeds of parliaments and armies for it seems quite clear that since the whole is greater than the part, he who writes of one small section cannot be as great as he who writes of nations and the world. Now and then there is a flash of sympathy for some Old Mortality chiseling afresh the epitaphs of years gone by, but he is usually dismissed with something of contempt as an antiquarian, uncritical and queer, in whose myopic vision perspective has no part and who painfully works out a futile record of the insignificant. If there is a spectacle more dreary than one of these, to the average man, it is a number of them gathered for mutual congratulation as a local historical society, for it is charged that their interest in the past is incidental to genealogy which itself grows out of snobbishness and vanity.[1]

Thus Dixon Ryan Fox described the once prevailing attitude in this country toward historical societies. What he probably did not realize at the time he wrote was that a large part of his relatively brief life would be devoted to the destruction of this popular myth. Perhaps no one in his generation did more to persuade Americans of the importance of the local incident in determining the general process of social evolution. Certainly, he convinced thousands of New Yorkers, during the quarter century after 1920, that if they desired to improve the environment in which they were living, they would have to do so out of knowledge of the way in which they had become what they were. Study of the records, physical and literary, of the shore, the valley, or the plateau where they lived would enrich associations of the hearthstone, making life more interesting and exciting. It would reveal, he insisted, the origins and growth of local institutions, as well as social groups, thus giving meaningful direction to continuing community activities. Only by an intelligent concern for their own history could any people put into proper perspective their natural concern about the future.

A Yorker born, Dixon Fox never escaped the spell of the Empire State. Its natural beauty—of forest, mountain, river, lake, and seashore—enthralled him. He loved to travel its rural roads, always seeking out the little-known byway. He was fascinated by its history, filled with high drama and stretching over three centuries since first the Dutch had found the North River, which others called the Hudson. To the interpretation of his own state's history, Fox brought enthusiasm and imagination and a remarkable facility in research. He had the ability, also, to make others realize the importance of the things that interested him. He knew all the clichés of the antiquarians, genealogists, museum curators, and spokesmen for local historical societies, but he rarely used them. If he did, he managed to give shopworn phrases an additional luster, as if brightly polished for his special purpose. Those who heard him speak were apt to find much that was novel in what should have been well-known.

Fox's preparation for the study and writing of history could not have been better had it been carefully planned in advance.

Dixon Ryan Fox

After receiving the diploma of the Normal School in Potsdam, New York, where he had been born on December 17, 1887, he taught school for several terms near Pleasantville in Westchester County. He entered Columbia College in New York City, graduating with the A.B. degree in 1911. At Columbia he quickly demonstrated his enthusiastic interest in American history and his untiring efforts to understand and interpret it. One of his classmates later remarked that he seemed to be the embodiment of unlimited energy, intelligently directed toward the exposition of historical data and the persuasion of his fellows to listen to him. He won the oratorical contest of the Philolexian Society and received a bronze replica of Houdon's famous bust of Washington, which he treasured as long as he lived. In the Varsity Show he had a show-stopping number with Edward Everett Horton, who went on to stop many a performance on Broadway and elsewhere. But chiefly he devoted his time to strenuous preparation for the advanced study of history in graduate school.

Fox gained the inspiration for much of his life's work from the faculty of political science at Columbia University. Here a goodly company of instructors helped him to "open windows and break down walls." Here he listened to the observations, often witty and sometimes profound, of that widely honored exemplar of the "New History," James Harvey Robinson; here he enjoyed, though often as a dissenter, Charles A. Beard's realistic appraisal of self-interest in the evolution of the American people; here he gained from William A. Dunning's conversation, more than from his lectures, new insight into the way in which the federal union had been saved, even at the tragic cost of civil strife. Probably no one in that company at Columbia so well exemplified the stereotype of the pedantic scholar as Herbert L. Osgood; yet from him Fox learned the invaluable lessons of painstaking research, which went so far to balance his own flair for the histrionic. In the years of his graduate study he earned not only the master's degree (1912) and the doctorate (1917) but also the opportunity to teach, first in Columbia College and later in the faculty of political science. It was the fulfillment of an ambition that went back to his student years.

In his doctoral dissertation, "The Decline of Aristocracy in the Politics of New York," Fox described the social forces that he believed had brought about the gradual democratization of political processes in New York State early in the nineteenth century. More readable than most dissertations written in American universities, his study revealed much of his own social and economic philosophy. Sensitive as he was to the need for a broad popular base for governmental institutions, he could not refrain from doubt that the overwhelming of the "tie-wig aristocracy" during the first half of the nineteenth century had been pure gain for the American people. Against the leveling tendencies of democracy, often capricious and strident in his own generation, he set the virtues of the earlier aristocratic tradition. Its social inequities he could not and would not condone; but in his mind's eye the great landed gentry had usually been the embodiment of "honor, magnanimity, steadiness and moral courage." He was inclined to let their seemly grace of manner compensate for a certain arrogant spirit that some of them regrettably manifested.

At the very beginning of his serious historical writing, Fox seemed to view the political scene, with its diplomatic intrigues and military conflicts, as a superficial evidence of powerful social and economic forces that required careful study in the local incident, if their general significance was to be understood. This attitude made him ready, indeed eager, to join Arthur Meier Schlesinger in a plan for a multi-volume, co-operative *History of American Life* that would elaborate on many of the germinal suggestions already made by Schlesinger in his *New Viewpoints in American History*. As the two editors conceived this enterprise, it would help "to free American history from its traditional

Dixon Ryan Fox

servitude to party struggles, war and diplomacy, and to show how it properly includes all the varied interests of the people."

In its final form, thirteen volumes completed in 1948, the *History* probably accomplished even more than Schlesinger had hoped for. It stimulated scholarly research and teaching in the social and cultural aspects of our history which had previously been neglected, and it helped to turn more and more graduate students toward specialization in the various phases of man's history that were outside the strictly political sphere. Although Fox was a junior partner in this scholarly work, his own thinking was deeply stirred by his collaboration with Arthur Schlesinger. In some ways the most convincing evidence of this comes from the paper, "A Synthetic Principle for Social History," which Fox read at the annual meeting of the American Historical Association in December, 1929.

His theme, richly furnished with striking illustrations, undertook to show how the social evolution of institutions, as well as professions, advanced from a sort of confused composite of functions to a more sharply defined limitation of function. The medical practitioners, for example, who once cut hair, pulled teeth, dispensed drugs, in addition to dabbling in every form of the healing art, slowly emerged over the centuries as diagnosticians, pathologists, surgeons, and a host of other specialists. So, too, the printer, who had once been a "multiple functionary" preparing copy, setting type, writing editorials, selling books, and conducting a small circulating library slowly became the progenitor of the reporter, the publisher, the editor, the book dealer, and the advertising agency. This process of differentiation, Fox argued, gave vitality to social history. It helped to make the works of the social historian something more than a series of panoramic culture pictures; it helped to make of them a living whole.

In many respects, this was the most significant contribution that Dixon Fox made to the study and writing of social history.

Keepers of the Past

It colored his thinking about the scope of the historian's interest and the techniques he should use in his research and his writing. It unquestionably affected the direction that he gave to the New York State Historical Association after he became its president in 1929. For a decade, he had been a member of the association, helping to arrange its programs, securing speakers for its annual meetings, recruiting new members, and writing scholarly papers subsequently printed in its quarterly journal.

When he accepted a position of leadership, the New York State Historical Association was still a society of intelligent amateurs who regarded history as an entertaining and important hobby. He was the first professional historian to be elected president, and he promptly moved to persuade academic historians to become interested in the association's work. In this, he was phenomenally successful. Without minimizing the good fellowship among members attending the annual meetings, without challenging the emphasis on local tradition and folklore, which some esteemed so highly, he enlisted a growing number of scholars as participants in the association's programs and gave substance to his claim that what had started as a hobby for a few had become a "sodality of adult education."

He was quick to support Alexander C. Flick, then state historian, in his task of editing a multivolume *History of the State of New York* that would rank with Folwell's *Minnesota* or A. B. Hart's *Massachusetts*. "The State of New York," Fox often remarked, "having a great history, deserves a good *History*." When the project ran into publication difficulties, he secured the generous assistance of Frederick Coykendall and Charles G. Proffitt of the Columbia University Press, and a first-rate ten-volume *History* appeared in pleasing format under the imprint of that press. At the same time, Fox gave to scores of local historical societies a new realization that the "little things" they were doing in their home communities constituted a significant part of the history of the Empire State.

Dixon Ryan Fox

The talent of the accomplished impresario marked Dixon Fox in many of his activities. Members of the historical association, whether they gathered at Southhampton or Lake Mohonk or Elmira or Chautauqua or Niagara Falls (and they met in every section of the state), came to expect something dramatic at each annual meeting. At Ticonderoga in September, 1933, the blare of trumpets and the roll of drums so stirred the imagination that one could see in the eye of fancy "savage warriors, dauntless brothers of the gray and black gowns, intrepid coureurs de bois, captains of old France, kilted Scots of the Black Watch, gay-clad grenadiers," and the whole host that had followed them into the wilderness of North America. Actually the scene, beneath the ramparts of old Fort Ticonderoga that bright September day, was a lively reconstruction of another age in New York's history, for the historical association welcomed hundreds of its friends from north of the Canadian border. There were the Fifth Royal Highlanders, long allied with the famous Black Watch, Chevaliers of Carillon, descendants of the Marquis de Chartier de Lotbiniére (military architect of the old fortress that guarded the Champlain-Hudson route), and representatives of historical societies from Montreal and Quebec. They had come to help dedicate a memorial to Lotbiniére on the spot where he had once bridged the stream that joins the waters of Lake Champlain and Lake George. That accomplished, they marched behind the pipers and drummers of the Highlanders to unveil a tablet on the South Bastion of Fort Ticonderoga, lately restored through the energy and generosity of Stephen Pell. Such pageantry fascinated Dixon Fox, and he knew well how to use it to stir his countrymen to an awareness of the high drama of their own history.

Not the least of his talents was his ability to transmit to others his deep concern for the preservation of the physical survivals from New York's past. He helped the Westchester County Historical Society establish a historical museum in the early eighteenth century Hammond House near Elmsford. He repeatedly reminded the readers of *New York History* of the houses in the state that were being neglected. The mansion built by John Peter De Lancey at Mamaroneck, after Heathcote Hall was destroyed in the revolution, looked humiliated as the front for a modern filling station. On Staten Island the famous Conference House, rich in memories of Benjamin Franklin's rebuff to General Howe, needed to be redeemed from its employment as a factory producing rat poison. These and others were perennial challenges to state and regional historical societies. Some of the sites were noble enough to be converted into museums that could portray the recurrent drama of our social history.

The president of the New York State Historical Association needed able lieutenants, and he got them. The four directors of the association since 1930 have been men of unusual ability. Three of them—Julian P. Boyd, Edward P. Alexander, and Clifford L. Lord—worked closely with President Fox, while the fourth, Louis C. Jones, carries on today at Cooperstown in the same fine tradition. During the Fox era, it would be appropriate to speak of the Boyds, the Alexanders, and the Lords, for in each instance the director's wife was an equal partner with him in making the association's program a success. Between Fox and his lieutenants there was always a fruitful exchange of ideas, which makes it difficult to determine precisely who proposed each item in the program of outstanding achievement.

This was the period in which the library at Ticonderoga rapidly expanded, filling most of the space in the beautiful Headquarters House, built along the lines of John Hancock's Boston home and given to the association by its first great benefactor, Horace Moses, a Yorker who never quite turned Yankee. These were the years when farm implements and utensils, arranged on the third floor of Headquarters House, became the nucleus of the magnificent Farmers' Museum, finally established in 1942 in the spacious and substantial barns on Fenimore Farm in

Dixon Ryan Fox

Cooperstown. This museum, as Jared Van Wagenen, Jr., Director Lord, and President Fox all pointed out, was not just another antiquarian venture. It was dedicated to the education of American youth, with exhibits so arranged that even the novice could see the complete process of manufacture in many a rural craft. It was calculated to give all visitors an understanding of the way in which the early farmstead had operated as a self-sufficient unit in American life. Meanwhile, Director Alexander had undertaken, with scholarly insight and administrative skill, the compilation of a sort of Doomsday Book of manuscript material relating to the history of the state. This led him into an important position with New York's Historical Records Survey, all of which could be set down to the credit of the association. Director Lord helped President Fox make plans to involve the younger generation in adventures in American history. These came to fruition when the association created a junior membership and began publication of the *Yorker*, which reached hundreds, then thousands, of secondary school students whose teachers had inspired them to form historical clubs.

The light that was shining with ever greater brilliance at Headquarters House in Ticonderoga and Central Quarters, later Fenimore House, in Cooperstown, was by no means hidden under the proverbial bushel. Newspapers were encouraged to devote more space to items of historical interest, and the association offered prizes each year to the journals that were most perceptive in the publication of historical material. Even more important in telling the association's story were the delightful vignettes by Charles Messer Stow of the New York *Sun*, which brought many an inquiry from his readers who desired to share in an enterprise at once so educational and so enjoyable.

Dixon Ryan Fox gave so much of himself to the historical association that it is difficult to realize this was only one of his many responsibilities. Until 1934, he was an energetic member of the faculty of political science at Columbia University, where he guided scores of students toward the doctorate in history, taught a full program of courses, directed the Summer Session as far as the history department was concerned, edited the *Columbia Quarterly* for several years, and imaginatively planned the celebration of the University's 175th anniversary in 1929. At the same time, he served on the Executive Council of the American Historical Association and was vice president of the Westchester County Historical Society, editing at its request *The Minutes of the Court of Sessions of Westchester County*.

His home on Fountain Terrace in Scarsdale, built at the close of the Mexican War, was itself something of an historic site. Here he and his wife, Marian Osgood, daughter of his early preceptor, Herbert L. Osgood, graciously welcomed Columbia University students and all others who were interested in the study, teaching, and writing of history. It was a spot he loved.

So happy was his association with Columbia University that he had misgivings when he was asked to become president of Union College in Schenectady in the spring of 1934. There had been other opportunities in college administration, but he was not interested in a position beyond the borders of the Empire State. At Union College he soon became an educational leader, known throughout the nation. His quick wit and eloquent phrases made him a popular speaker at many public ceremonies. New York University named him Anson G. Phelps Lecturer and published his lectures under the title *Yankee and Yorker* (1940). Union College, he insisted, always came first; yet he found time to continue his vigorous leadership of the historical association. Indeed, it was Union College business that brought him acquaintance with Stephen C. Clark of Cooperstown, who hoped to make the little village on Lake Otsega (James Fenimore Cooper's "Glimmerglass") a center of historical research based on a first-rate historical museum and library of New York history. Clark's generous vision and Fox's ingenuity combined to give the historical association new dimensions. Headquarters

Dixon Ryan Fox

House at Ticonderoga was matched in 1939 by Central Quarters, later by Fenimore House on Lake Otsega. For more than three years, Fox and Clark were an irresistible team with the assistance of Director Alexander. When Alexander resigned (1941) to become director of the Wisconsin Historical Society, he was succeeded by Clifford Lord, like his predecessor a graduate of Columbia University. Fox was proud of the honors bestowed on his lieutenants and pleased that they always trained an excellent administrative staff. For example, when Lord became an officer in the United States Navy, Miss Mary Cunningham and Miss Janet McFarlane at Cooperstown and Mrs. Lape at Ticonderoga maintained the pace and the standards to which New Yorkers had become accustomed.

Plans were underway for new activities in the association when death came suddenly to Dixon Ryan Fox (January 30, 1945) at high noon of his career. The demands upon him had been so great, so varied were the interests that commanded his attention, that his effectiveness as scholar, teacher, and educational administrator might have been impaired, but this did not happen. His whole contribution to his generation could be fittingly described in Browning's well-known lines:

> Who keeps one end in view
> Makes all things serve.

SOURCES AND NOTE

The Decline of Aristocracy in the Politics of New York (New York, 1965) contains a biographical sketch of Dixon Ryan Fox written by Robert V. Remini. Other biographical data appear in the obituary notice in *The New York Times,* Jan. 31, 1945. Much of Dr. Fox's philosophy concerning historical societies is explicit in "The President's Page," which he wrote for each issue of *New York History* from January, 1930, to September, 1944. His most important contributions as a social historian were published under the title, *Ideas in Motion* (New York, 1935).

1. Quoted in *New York History* XXIII (1942), p. 9, but written by Fox much earlier.

II. The Public Archive

John Franklin Jameson

by David D. Van Tassel

"Fate," wrote John Franklin Jameson, "has prevented me from ever writing a history, and confined me to the simple role of a powder monkey, passing forward ammunition for others to fire off."[1] Although he wrote a good deal, Jameson's achievements as a historian are based not on his writings but on his great success in promoting American historical scholarship through personal contacts and correspondence, through his work in the American Historical Association, and as editor of the *American Historical Review* through most of the period from its founding in 1895 until 1928.

His professional functions are a matter of record, but his efforts in discovering, collecting, preserving, and editing the materials for American history, if not more important, are at once more tangible yet less well known. He was the initiator, first chairman, and general editor of the American Historical Association's Historical Manuscripts Commission (1895-96), which located and published in the volumes of the *Annual Report* papers of public figures which were privately-owned. He initiated and planned the long-term program of the Bureau (later Department) of Historical Research of the Carnegie Institution of Washington (1903), serving as "chief" or director from 1905 until 1928. Jameson, more than any other single man, is responsible for the organization and centralization of federal records in the National Archives Building, as well as the establishment of the National Historical Publications Commission. He promoted the government publication of many important documents, including the huge series of *Territorial Papers of the United States*.[2] He, along with his able protégé, Waldo G. Leland, deserves most of the credit for establishing the Public Archives Commission of the American Historical Association, which spurred the movement to establish state archives commissions and laid the foundations for the new profession of archivist. From 1921 to 1926, Jameson shouldered most of the burden of raising funds for the publication of the *Dictionary of American Biography,* one of the first projects of the new American Council of Learned Societies. In 1928, when he moved to the newly established "Chair of American History" in the Library of Congress and became chief of the Division of Manuscripts of the Library, he expanded the library's project for photocopying materials for American history in foreign collections. The list goes on and on, but this is sufficient to establish his significance as "a keeper of records."

J. Franklin Jameson (as he was known in professional circles) was a man of imposing appearance as well as reputation—a living stereotype of the New England gentleman-scholar. He was tall and lean with reddish-brown hair, parted in the middle and turning grey at the temples. His prim, rimless spectacles perched on a straight nose separating precise grey eyes. His full mustache, descending to meet a close-cut beard trimmed to an exquisite point, added to the stiff formality of his habitually austere expression. He gave the appearance of a Boston aristocrat born and bred, with fingerbowl manners and a stern morality as rigid and straight as his own backbone.

Jameson's friends, however, saw a different man, revealed by "frequent warm and friendly smiles." He liked people and basked in the companionship of good friends. He would bring together groups of congenial people on the slightest pretext, forming ephemeral organizations such as the "Nucleus," so named because it was the nucleus of nothing. Since his graduate days, he frequently enjoyed "fiery discussions," at the dinner table and after, on any topic—"theology and politics, immortality and second marriages." He enjoyed music and played the flute, read poetry and wrote letters. Oh, the letters! He must have enjoyed this most of all, for he wrote voluminously and well to all kinds of people, high and low, all over the world.

He had an impish sense of humor and a knack for light verse.

> Tis sweet, in moods of exaltation,
>   To read the proof of archive-guides;
> To mend defects of punctuation
>   A supersensual joy provides—
> To seize the comma where it hides
>   And see its force aright displayed,
> And swift invoke, with happy stroke,
>   The modest semi-colon's aid.[3]

He once wrote to Edward G. Lowry, editor of the *Saturday Evening Post,* just after the Mexican Revolution of 1911, suggesting that Mexico call for the services of Colonel Roosevelt as president. He would "make Mexico hum" while, Jameson added, "this would solve several difficulties in this city and elsewhere in the United States."[4]

This sense of whimsey, which lightens Jameson's letters, gave him a perspective on himself, his work, and the work of other scholars. It also reveals a sympathetic understanding of people and a warmth that belies the cold face of Victorian rectitude staring out of formal portraits.

J. Franklin Jameson in many ways typifies the transition in the historical profession that took place at the *fin de siècle.*

Keepers of the Past

The era of great amateurs was ending. Jameson was born in 1859 at the height of the period when literary historians and collectors, often scions of "old" families with some wealth, wrote on subjects that interested them for their intrinsic dramatic and literary possibilities, or who collected materials of ancestral or local interest. In 1882, when Jameson received the first doctoral degree awarded by Johns Hopkins, the new age of the professionally-trained, card-carrying Ph.D. was just beginning. He was in the vanguard of an army of Ph.D.'s who would flood the colleges and the universities, infiltrating the historical societies and organizing the archives, all in the name of Science.

Jameson grew up in an atmosphere of poverty and learning in Boston where his father, John, taught at the Boyleston School. Brilliant and gifted with an extremely retentive memory, young Franklin was admitted to Harvard at fifteen. Meanwhile the Boyleston school had closed, and straitened circumstances forced the young student to work in a store and to live with his grandparents. Perhaps under their influence, he first experienced the excitement of historical discovery as he followed maternal family lines from the timeworn lettering on gravestones to dusty ill-kept town records. Archives!

After his freshman year, the family moved west to Amherst, and Franklin, much against his will, transferred to Amherst College. Though he won prizes in five other fields, he never wavered from his initial determination to devote his life to the study of history.

Finances prevented his making what was at that time the obligatory pilgrimage to Europe to obtain the German Ph.D., and in the autumn of 1880, after a disappointing year teaching high school, he enrolled in the new graduate school in Baltimore, The Johns Hopkins University. Two years later, at the age of twenty-three, he received his Ph.D., and began nineteen years of teaching at "Hopkins" and later (1888-1901) at Brown University. In April, 1901, he became chairman of the department of history at the University of Chicago. Once again, he had made a major decision reluctantly, persuaded, "much against my will," by the dynamic William Rainey Harper and the challenge of the West he disdained.

Although by all accounts he did well in building up an active history faculty, he did not like Chicago, and in 1905 leaped at the opportunity to return east as director of the Bureau of Historical Research of the Carnegie Institution of Washington and to reassume his duties as editor of the *American Historical Review*. He continued in both capacities until 1928, when he resigned in the face of imminent forced retirement and dissolution of the bureau. He then moved immediately into the new "Chair of American History" and the position of chief of the Division of Manuscripts in the Library of Congress, both of which he held until his death in September, 1937.

In these years, Jameson did too much, inspired too many programs, to catalog in a short essay. Even the three major areas of his work included in this account can only be broadly sketched. The first of these areas, to which he devoted much of his life, was the collection and preservation of manuscripts important to American history. However, simply accumulating sources, as he well knew, is only a first step. Therefore, he devoted himself also to making source materials known and accessible to historians. But, he discovered, in order to accomplish anything of national significance in the first two fields, he would have to enter still a third. This came to involve all the techniques of propaganda, promotion, public relations, and lobbying, in a campaign to educate public officials and historians to the urgent need for systematic collection, preservation, and organization of manuscripts, particularly in public archives. It produced, among other accomplishments, a National Archives Building, the National Archives Act of 1934, and the development of a new profession—archivist.

The first requisite for a "scientific" history of the country was the availability of all possible primary sources—manuscript records, documents, and correspondence. Jameson saw the need —as had many other historians—and in 1891, he publicly launched a lifelong campaign for the systematic collection, organization, and publication of these source materials for American history. He studied the nature of European archives and compared the expenditures of foreign governments for history with those of the United States. The latter suffered by comparison, not in funds expended but in results, both in quantity and quality. He announced his conclusions to historians in December, 1891, at the Washington meeting of the American Historical Association and suggested that the association urge Congress to establish a National Historical Manuscripts Commission sufficiently endowed and staffed by scholars to accomplish the herculean task that lay ahead.[5]

Jameson had no illusions as to the difficulties involved in persuading Congress to finance such a project. He had already suffered his first defeat in an earlier effort to persuade Congress to publish the records of the Virginia Company. In his opinion, the only hope lay with the federal government or the association; for he held low regard, if not contempt, for erratic amateurs, as well as most state and local historical societies.[6]

But even the national organization of professional historians failed him. The American Historical Association took no action on his suggestion for a National Historical Manuscripts Commission. Jameson, far from forsaking the project, waited to seize the right moment. The time came four years later (1895) when he joined a successful and genteel palace revolt in the association against the one-man rule of Herbert Baxter Adams, his former teacher. A rejuvenated council authorized, for the first time in the life of the association, a standing committee—the Historical Manuscripts Commission—appointed Jameson chairman, and appropriated a $500 budget.

The commission, modeling its program after that of the

John Franklin Jameson

British Royal Historical Manuscripts Commission, proposed to locate, calendar, and print historical manuscripts of national significance in private hands which were not likely to be placed in public depositories. However, it never followed the proposed policy. Jameson sought out such materials, particularly for his edition of the Calhoun papers,[7] but the commission never made a systematic effort to locate collections of papers in private hands, nor did it publish any extensive calendar of manuscripts. Instead, during the forty years of its existence, the commission published a huge quantity and variety of documents and manuscripts, as volumes of the *Annual Reports*: portions of the correspondence of Bayard, Hunter, Combs, Stephens, and Cobb, Martin Van Buren's *Autobiography, The Diplomatic Correspondence of the Republic of Texas,* and a great deal more.[8]

The commission's work quickly accentuated the differences between private papers and public archives. In 1899, the association recognized the distinction by establishing a separate Public Archives Commission, which promoted and published surveys of records in the archives of forty states. It launched an intensive propaganda campaign to secure legislation to establish state archives commissions and succeeded in a number of states, particularly in the South.[9]

In 1909, at the initiative of Waldo G. Leland, Jameson's chief protégé, Jameson and the members of the Public Archives Commission organized the annual Conference of Archivists, a semiautonomous section of the American Historical Association. The conference was the first self-conscious body of archivists in the United States, and its founding marks the beginning of a new profession. The archivists, relatively satisfied with the annual conference, did not consolidate their position into a separate professional organization until 1937, when they dissolved the conference and founded the Society of American Archivists.

Jameson would scarcely claim credit for the founding of the archival profession in the United States, but he does deserve some of the responsibility, because it was through his work and under his tutelage as Director of the Department of Historical Research of the Carnegie Institution that many men, such as Waldo Leland, first received their training in, and their introduction to, archival problems.

If Jameson helped to train archivists, he would say that it was merely a fortunate by-product of the major work of the department, but even the Department of Historical Research owed its very existence to Jameson, for he not only headed it during the years of its greatest productivity, shaping its program, but had planned and initiated its organization. The idea grew out of a plan suggested by Frederick Jackson Turner for a historical school for graduate students at Washington. A few months after Jameson moved from Brown to Chicago (1901), he heard that Herbert Baxter Adams, who had recently died, had left the American Historical Association a bequest of $5,000. Jameson immediately wrote to the council suggesting that the funds be used to found such a school. The council appointed a committee consisting of Jameson, James Ford Rhodes (declined, and Charles Francis Adams, Jr., appointed), and Andrew C. McLaughlin. Jameson was already in contact with Daniel Coit Gilman, who was then planning and organizing a similar school for scientists, which Andrew Carnegie had already become interested in financing. Jameson's New England reserve scarcely contained his intense excitement at the prospect. He wrote to Gilman in February, 1902: "I have found myself so warmly interested in the project of the Carnegie Institution and in the question of what it might do for history, that I conclude to be emboldened by your letter of some time ago to set before you a lot of suggestions...."[10] And he did.

The outcome of much correspondence, planning, and work was the establishment of the Bureau of Historical Research of the Carnegie Institution of Washington in March, 1903, with Andrew C. McLaughlin as director. Jameson, who had been counting on the position, was bitterly disappointed. "All the disagreements of my present position...and all the discomforts of life in this lonely and hideous town, were pretty easily borne, under the constant thought that I should soon be out of it."[11] And, by 1905, he was "out of it," for upon the resignation of McLaughlin he assumed the position that he had planned for himself.

It is difficult to estimate the service that the Carnegie Institution rendered to historical studies during Jameson's tenure. The tangible results alone are impressive. Jameson raised the annual budget for history from $12,000 in 1905 to $42,000 in 1927 —his own salary of $5,000 remaining unchanged. Jameson, and McLaughlin before him, sent scholars to most of the major archives of Europe to search out and describe materials relating to American history. The institution published or subsidized publication of at least forty volumes, including twenty-two guides to sources for American history in archives that stretched from the West Indies to Russia, and edited volumes of documents, such as Leo Stock's five-volume *Proceedings and Debates of the British Parliament Respecting North America, 1542 to 1754* and John Spencer Bassett's seven-volume edition of the correspondence of Andrew Jackson.

The guides, many of them superficial and no longer adequate, still remain essential tools, though the calendaring of the most important collections that Jameson had projected was jettisoned when the trustees of the Carnegie Institution forced his retirement and the dissolution of the department. Even so, the guides have been extremely important, both to American historians and to the Library of Congress in its efforts to collect transcripts and later photocopies of material relating to America's past from European depositories.[12]

Fortunately for Jameson and for historical studies in America, he was able to carry out a large portion of the master plan. Hearing that he was to be retired at seventy, he resigned (1928)

Keepers of the Past

to accept the post of chief of the Division of Manuscripts of the Library of Congress. Although angered and disappointed, he told his friends and former staff: "I can only do as Perry did on Lake Erie.... Namely, if my flagship is going to be shot to pieces, I shall simply take my flag over to another ship and keep on with the fight."[13] And that is just what he did. He "kept on with the fight" by pushing forward three major projects.

The first was the photocopying of material from European archives respecting American history, financed by John D. Rockefeller, Jr., and initiated by Samuel Flagg Bemis in 1923. Aided by his guide series and his own vast knowledge of the archives of Europe, he was able to bring to the Library of Congress an immense body of material. The second, over which Jameson had general supervision, included *A Census of Medieval and Renaissance Manuscripts in the United States,* edited by Seymour de Ricci, and *A Catalog of Latin and Vernacular Alchemical Manuscripts in the United States and Canada,* edited by William Jerome Wilson. The third was the creation of a national archives and public records program centered in the National Archives Building, which would be the greatest physical monument to J. Franklin Jameson.

Many men and departments of the government had been conscious of the need for better maintenance and administration of our national archives before Jameson arrived at the front. In 1877, President Hayes transmitted to Congress the report of a commission appointed to consider the security of the public buildings of Washington against fire, proposing "that a fireproof building...be constructed for the accommodation of the archives of the government...."[14] But Congress did nothing, even under the constant and yearly pleas that were hidden deep in the jungle of words and pages of heavy reports from executive bureau heads and cabinet members.

The American Historical Association entered the fight in 1901 when it endorsed a joint proposal of federal departments for a

John Franklin Jameson

National Hall of Records. Jameson did not join the battle actively until 1908, when he was appointed chairman of the association's committee to promote the movement for an archives building in Washington. From that time on, through February 20, 1933, when President Hoover laid the cornerstone of the building, and June 19, 1934, when President Roosevelt finally approved the National Archives Act, Jameson led the battle, rallying his conglomerate forces after each defeat and constantly enlisting new supporters. He corresponded with the secretary of the treasury and various members of the Senate, petitioned President Taft, drafted bills for Congress, and circularized the historical societies of the country. He addressed the Daughters of the American Revolution and the American Library Association to gain their support. He obtained newspaper and periodical publicity: the *Review of Reviews,* the *Nation,* the New York *Evening Post,* the *Washington Star*—all presented graphic accounts of existing conditions, most of them using materials supplied by Jameson and his aides. President Taft, in 1910, made a futile effort to urge Congress to meet the need for such a building. By 1913, most supporters were encouraged as Woodrow Wilson, a historian and scholar, entered the White House, but Jameson was not optimistic. We shall see "whether an executive order 'Let there be archives, W. Wilson,' will be potent with the sixty-third Congress. I am afraid when it should get through to them it would emerge in the shape of 'Let them archives be.' "[15] Wilson was not interested in the project. Toward the end of 1916, Jameson nearly lost hope, as the Democrats continued in control. He wrote to McLaughlin with insight (if not partisanship), "Republicans are a little more interested in things like good filing systems."[16] Jameson proved to be correct.

After the Great War, he renewed the attack. In 1921, he seized upon a fire in the Census Records to attract public attention to his cause. He wrote several Senators, lamenting the fire but cheerfully pointing out that it was not unique since, between

1833 and 1915, some 254 fires had occurred in buildings used by the United States government.[17] The American Legion entered the fray because of its interest in the veterans' records. By November, 1921, Jameson's enthusiasm mounted as he told friends that now they might get somewhere, "if somebody can make a noise like public opinion." Congress did pass an enabling act but conveniently failed to appropriate the necessary funds. In 1923, the Hearst newspapers joined the campaign. Jameson declared that he would fight till the death and that he expected to hammer at this matter "until the undertaker hammers the lid over me."[18]

President Coolidge, who received Jameson's persistent presidential briefing on archives, turned out to be not only more receptive but more effective. His message in 1926, including a curt request for the establishment of an archives building, moved Congress not only to pass a bill, May 25, 1926, but to appropriate the money necessary to buy the land, design the building, and pay for its completion. After many more tribulations and delays, construction officially started on February 20, 1933, when President Hoover laid the cornerstone. In 1934, Congress passed the National Archives Act that provided for the new office of archivist of the United States and defined his powers and duties. Upon signing the legislation on June 19, President Franklin Roosevelt sought Jameson's advice as to the proper man for the position. Jameson, with the support of the American Historical Association, urged the appointment of R. D. W. Connor, founder and former secretary of the North Carolina Historical Commission.

In his old age, Jameson was *the* "historical statesman" to whom archivists, historians, and leaders all over the world turned for advice. He sternly criticized the ever-lengthening Ph.D. dissertation, which he often proclaimed should not run over a hundred pages because any more tended to kill the student's ability if not his enthusiasm for writing. Jameson

John Franklin Jameson

deplored the poor literary quality of most historical articles and monographs just as often and vehemently as he criticized haphazard or purely antiquarian collecting. The work of collecting and preserving documents and making them accessible to scholars was continued and, although he always emphasized those materials of national importance, he did not limit himself to collecting orthodox sources but sought out the materials for new fields of history. He championed the study of religious history and sponsored a project to locate and preserve pertinent papers in a day of political history. The collection of industrial and business records, as well as the records of Negro history in America, was urged by Jameson. He cultivated social history long before it became the vogue, delivering six lectures at Barnard in 1895, in which he set forth an economic and social interpretation of the American Revolution. He did not publish these essays, however, until 1926, when he refurbished the notes for another series he gave at Princeton University, and they were printed there under the title, *The American Revolution Considered as a Social Movement.* Charles A. Beard immediately hailed the book as "a challenge to windbags.... A truly notable book.... Studded with novel illustrative materials, gleaming with new illumination...." Jameson was pleased; nevertheless, he took impish glee in informing "my dear Mr. Beard" of the date when he first composed the "new" social and economic interpretation of the revolution.[19]

This little volume was his most mature monograph and the closest he ever came to writing "a history." Instead, he devoted his life, as he told Henry Adams, to "making bricks without much idea of how the architects will use them, but believing that the best architect that ever was cannot get along without bricks, and therefore trying to make good ones."[20] Some historians have praised, and more will come to, his success in "making bricks," but others, hopelessly lost among the piles of documentary "bricks" housed in fireproof buildings or entangled in thousands of feet of microfilm, with no possibility of relief through fire, destruction, or loss, may mildly curse in an unguarded moment, even in the National Archives Building, the success of J. Franklin Jameson as a keeper of the records of the American past.

SOURCES AND NOTES

The basic source is the Jameson Papers, including his diary, in the Library of Congress. For the most part, the only letters cited are those that are printed in the excellently annotated selection, *An Historian's World: Selections from the Correspondence of John Franklin Jameson*, Elizabeth Donnan and Leo F. Stock, eds. [*Memoirs* of the American Philosophical Society, XLII] (Philadelphia, 1956). There is no book-length biography of Jameson; but see Elizabeth Donnan's introduction to *Historian's World*, 1-17, and Waldo G. Leland, "John Franklin Jameson," *D.A.B.*, 2nd supplement (New York, 1958), 339-44. His collecting and archival work are thoroughly covered in John Beverley Riggs, "The Acquisition of Foreign Archival Material for American History, to the year 1940" (Ph.D. dissertation, Yale, 1955).

1. Jameson to Wilbur C. Abbott, Oct. 6, 1924. Quoted in Elizabeth Donnan and Leo F. Stock, eds., *An Historian's World: Selections from the Correspondence of John Franklin Jameson* [*Memoirs* of the American Philosophical Society, XLII] (Philadelphia, 1956), p. 302.
2. Clarence E. Carter, ed. (Washington, D.C., 1934-56), 22 vols.
3. John Franklin Jameson, "An Editor's Farewell," read at a dinner given in his honor in New York, Feb. 24, 1928. Quoted in Donnan and Stock, *Historian's World*, p. 302.
4. Jameson to Lowry, Feb. 26, 1912, *ibid.*, p. 147.
5. Jameson, "Expenditure of Foreign Governments for History," *Annual Report* of the American Historical Association for 1891 (Washington, D.C., 1892), pp. 33-61.
6. He once declared with youthful superiority that "our naive grandfathers' ideas of what is necessary to preserve are to us as the poke bonnets and spinning wheels of all old garrets" (Jameson, *History of Historical Writing in America* [Boston, 1891], p. 88; also see Jameson, "The Functions of State and Local Historical Societies with Respect to Research and Publication," *Annual Report* [1897], pp. 53-59). Years later Jameson elaborated upon his earlier position in answer to a question from an official of the New-York Historical Society. He pointed out that the eastern historical societies often fell into the hands of rich old men with little to do, men who had little sense of values in history or in the present.

John Franklin Jameson

A man of this sort, Jameson declared, "views the world from his club window, he interests himself in small antiquarian objects—liberty poles and regimental buttons.... Often he cares about nothing subsequent to the Revolution, which seventy or a hundred years ago, when some of these societies were founded, was an allowable *terminus ad quem...*" (Jameson to Alexander J. Wall, Jan. 31, 1923, Donnan and Stock, *Historian's World*, p. 284).

7. "The Correspondence of John C. Calhoun," J. F. Jameson, ed., *Annual Report*, II (1899).

8. "Report of the Historical Manuscripts Commission," *Annual Report*, I (1896), 467-80; *Ibid*. (1897), 399-403, and succeeding yearly reports through 1934; Lucile M. Kane, "Manuscript Collecting," in William B. Hesseltine and Donald R. McNeil, eds., *In Support of Clio* (Madison, Wis., 1958), pp. 29-48.

9. David D. Van Tassel, "The American Historical Association in the South, 1884-1913," *Journal of Southern History*, XXIII (Nov., 1957), 476-77.

10. Jameson to Gilman, Feb. 14, 1902, Donnan and Stock, *Historian's World*, p. 79.

11. Jameson to Francis A. Christie, Mar. 6, 1903, *ibid.*, pp. 85-86.

12. "Report of the Advisory Committee on History," Carnegie Institution of Washington, *Yearbook*, I, 1901-1902 (Washington, D.C., 1903), 226-31; also a summary of work done to 1927 in Jameson, "Report of the Department of Historical Research," *ibid.*, XXVI, 1927-28 (Washington, D.C., 1929), 89-97.

13. Jameson to Elizabeth Donnan, Nov. 14, 1927, in Jameson Papers, Division of Manuscripts, Library of Congress; and an excellent account of Jameson's work and that of others is John Beverley Riggs, "The Acquisition of Foreign Archival Sources for American History to the year 1940," (Ph.D. dissertation, Yale, 1955), especially 169-295.

14. Report of the President's "Commission on the security of Public Buildings in Washington against Fire," to Congress, 1877, in G. Philip Bauer, "Public Archives in the United States," in Hesseltine and McNeil, *In Support of Clio*, p. 64.

15. Jameson to Leland, Jan. 14, 1913, Donnan and Stock, *Historian's World*, p. 15.

16. Jameson to McLaughlin, Nov. 20, 1916, *ibid.*, 202; also see Jameson to Woodrow Wilson, Nov. 15, 1916, *ibid.*, 201-2; a detailed account of the long struggle to obtain a National Archives Building is in Fred Shelley's, "The Interest of J. Franklin Jameson in the National Archives, 1908-1934," *American Archivist*, XII (Apr., 1949), 99-130.

17. Jameson to John S. Bassett, Nov., 1921, Donnan and Stock, *Historian's World*, p. 16.

18. Jameson to Worthington C. Ford, Jan. 22, 1923, *ibid.*, p. 16.
19. Review of Jameson, "The American Revolution Considered as a Social Movement, Princeton University, 1926," *New Republic*, XLVII (Aug. 11, 1926), 344; Jameson to Beard, Aug. 10, 1926, Donnan and Stock, *Historian's World*, p. 319.
20. Jameson to Henry Adams, Oct. 31, 1910, Donnan and Stock, *ibid.*, p. 136.

Thomas McAdory Owen, Sr.

by James F. Doster

One of the first to see the need for state action in preserving our state and local historical records and to do something about it was Thomas McAdory Owen. It was he who originated the concept of a state department of archives and history and he who created the prototype in 1901 in his native Alabama. Owen's accomplishment did not come suddenly but was the work of a lifetime.

On December 15, 1866, when the State of Alabama was only forty-seven years old, Owen was born in Jonesboro, near present Bessemer. There were coal seams under the ground not far away, and Red Mountain's outcropping iron ore was to be seen, but there was no railroad within thirty miles. Birmingham and Bessemer were unheard of. When the crossing of two railroad lines in 1871 marked the site of Birmingham, the future iron and steel center, he was old enough to watch. What his meditations were as he grew up we do not know, but he came of a self-respecting and proud family and received a good early education. Young Owen was what may be called an early bloomer. In 1884, he entered the sophomore class of the University of Alabama at Tuscaloosa, just as that institution's intellectual and physical features were undergoing a notable improvement. He became sophomore orator, junior orator, Shakespearian prize man, Philomathic orator, captain of Company C of cadets, and editor-in-chief of the *University Monthly*. In his senior year, he took the law course. In 1887, at the age of twenty-one, he emerged with both A.B. and LL.B. degrees, scholastically first in his class of twenty-two.

Two months later, we find him engaged in the practice of law in the new coal and iron town of Bessemer. Already he was showing finely developed talents as a letter writer. His style was somewhat ornate, but his sentences were clear and complete, and the thought was well developed. In 1888, he became a justice of the peace; in 1889, president of the Alumni Society of the University of Alabama; in 1890, chairman of the Democratic executive committee of Jefferson County and city solicitor of Bessemer; and, in 1892, assistant solicitor of Jefferson County. He wrote to ask Congressman John H. Bankhead for the hand of his daughter, Marie, and on April 12, 1893, married into a family that for the next generation was one of the most prominent and influential in Alabama.

The career in which Owen attained his real distinction began as a side interest. In 1889, he was writing letters seeking complete collections of student publications of his *alma mater* and of the Sigma Nu Fraternity, of which he was a member. He sought books and documents relating to his native state and its history, then manuscripts, as his interests widened and his collection grew. Gradually realizing how little historical work had been done in the state, he resolved to write a full and comprehensive history of it,[1] but there was no large library available for such work. He gathered old newspapers, pamphlets, early maps, charts and prints, local and county histories, scrapbooks, private papers and correspondence, and histories of all the states bordering on Alabama.

After experiencing some financial difficulties, Owen asked his father-in-law to get him a government position, and on Septem-

Thomas McAdory Owen, Sr.

ber 1, 1894, arrived in Washington with the title of chief clerk of the Division of Post Office Inspectors and Mail Depredations. The work was not uninteresting, but it occupied him only from nine A.M. to four P.M., and his real preoccupation was with reading and continuing his historical collecting and genealogical studies. He wrote hundreds of letters to people in all parts of the country in search of materials for his collection on Alabama history. He became acquainted with kindred spirits throughout the United States and came to know intimately dozens of directors of historical societies and professors of history. He was eager to collect everything relating to his native state and region. He even wrote to several of his former professors, saying "kindly send me all of the old examination papers prepared by me while in your classes." His tastes were not catholic; they were merely undiscriminating. Yet, if he had tried to be selective, he would have discarded great quantities of materials of unsuspected value. He had just the right qualities of mind and character to serve the most critical historical need of his time. Among these were a persuasive and urbane personality, a helpful and kindly nature, and unbounded enthusiasm. He made and retained friends easily. Like a horse in green clover, he eagerly devoured the historical and intellectual resources of Washington. Especially valuable was the Library of Congress, headed by Dr. Ainsworth R. Spofford, who deeply influenced Owen.[2]

As a collector, compiler, bibliographer, and organizer Owen belongs in the top rank of the historical tribe. Yet he suffered some severe disappointments by misjudging his own abilities. Although highly literate and articulate, he lacked some of the qualities of a successful historical writer, and he seems to have taken offense at those publishers' criticisms that nearly all successful writers have endured and profited from. When he wrote a school history of Alabama and sent it to a publisher, he was gently told that it was "rather dry and statistical" and given advice as to how to rewrite it.[3] The publisher's requirements were soon met by a manuscript written not by Owen but by William Garrott Brown. Owen persisted in regarding history as something to be accumulated.

While in Washington, in 1896, he joined with other southerners, including several of national reputation, in forming the Southern History Association, of which he became the first treasurer. The organization flourished for a time and issued several volumes of *Publications*.

Tiring of Washington work, Owen decided he would like a professorship at the University of Alabama. He wrote to members of the board of trustees of that institution, saying he did not apply for any special place but would "undertake any one of the chairs of history, English, ancient or modern languages." He felt his qualifications to be "of the highest order."[4] Brashly naïve though these letters were, Owen had something to offer that is clear only in retrospect, for he was pioneering in something new. We can now read new meaning into his words: "If chosen to a chair, I shall make myself a credit to the institution, will devote all my energies to its upbuilding."[5] He did not get the job.

Owen's first important work in print was his "Bibliography of Alabama," published in the *Annual Report* of the American Historical Association for 1897. Then came his "Bibliography of Mississippi" in the *Annual Report* for 1899. These works are still quite valuable to scholars. They won for him a national reputation as a bibliographer, and he became increasingly prominent in the affairs of the American Historical Association.

Owen had meanwhile returned to Alabama and established a law practice in the little Black Belt town of Carrollton, but he was concerned more with history than with law. He had seen the potentialities of a state historical society in the work of Lyman C. Draper in Wisconsin, where the society was supported by the state. Reuben Gold Thwaites had explained the very successful institutional structure there in the same volume in which Owen's "Bibliography of Alabama" had been published. An

Thomas McAdory Owen, Sr.

Alabama Historical Society had been incorporated by the legislature on February 5, 1852, and, after sporadic periods of activity, it remained in suspended animation. It gave Owen a basis, however flimsy, on which to build.

Before he left Washington, Owen had prepared a bill to provide for a state commission to study the public and private records of Alabama history and to make recommendations concerning their preservation, but the legislature had taken no action.[6]

In response to Owen's persuasive urging, a meeting of the Alabama Historical Society was held at the university commencement in June, 1898. The society elected Governor Joseph Forney Johnston president and Thomas McAdory Owen secretary and chose an impressive executive committee and slate of officers.[7] The society, *alias* Owen, then began an active career. The secretary, without compensation, gave a large part of his time to the society's work. Writing letters by the hundreds, publishing appeals in newspapers, and seeking support everywhere that he could think of, Owen generated an impressive response. In the first year he sent out 1,515 letters, 631 circulars, and 40 postal cards, and he added 279 names to the membership roll. He edited a volume of the society's *Transactions* for 1897-98, started the collection of a society library through donations, persuaded several state newspapers to contribute regular complimentary copies to the library, promoted commemorations of historic events, wrote several papers for publication in the *Transactions,* and sought to start a historical journal.[8]

At Owen's urging, the legislature appropriated $250 a year, for two years, for the publication of the *Transactions* and passed an act authorizing an Alabama Historical Commission, made up of five members of the society, to "make a full, detailed and exhaustive examination of all the sources and materials, manuscript, documentary and record of the history of Alabama from the earliest times" and to report to the next session of the legisla-

{ 101 }

ture.[9] Owen became chairman of the new commission and served without compensation.

He moved to Birmingham in 1900 and took the headquarters of the historical society with him. University members of the executive committee were replaced with Birmingham men. Hoping to forestall the move, a committee of Tuscaloosa citizens, presumably with Owen's encouragement, tried to get the university trustees to establish a chair of Alabama historiography for him, but the trustees did not act.[10] In Birmingham, however, there were men of wealth who, under Owen's persuasion might contribute support, and he hoped through the aid of private contributions to secure a fireproof building and employ a staff. Yet before this plan could mature, he moved in another direction.

As chairman of the Alabama Historical Commission, Owen engaged in an active correspondence with persons and institutions by the hundreds, seeking information about historical records and also about other historical societies and how they functioned. He surveyed the field thoroughly to learn what others had done and to determine what was best for Alabama. One problem that troubled him was that of preserving public records, which were deteriorating from neglect and want of proper storage in state offices, county court houses, and city halls. He was deeply shocked to find a volume of original state papers of the Civil War period being used on the floor of the state capitol to hold a door open. Historical societies in other states did not seem to have any means of getting at this problem.

Owen sent a printed form letter to county and city officials in the state, calling for detailed information on public records, as the law allowed him to do. Despite the work that this imposed on the officials, he got a very good response. His report, which when later printed filled nearly 450 pages, was ready on schedule, in December, 1900.

Probably the most important thing in the report was its

recommendations. It urged further state support of the Alabama Historical Society and the establishment of a state department of archives and history, "charged with the custody of the State official archives, and collection and creation of a State library, museum and art gallery, with particular reference to the history and antiquities of Alabama, to be under the supervision of a Director" and with "a liberal continuing appropriation." The collections of the historical society were to be turned over to the new department, to form the nucleus of its collections. This plan "would place Alabama in the front rank" with those states that took "an intelligent interest in their history and archives." Beyond sentimental and patriotic considerations, the department would "prove of greatest practical benefit." The state archives would be given the care befitting their priceless value, and they would be arranged and indexed for immediate consultation by interested parties. The department would build "a great reference historical library" for the state. It would "also gather together the surviving letters and papers of our public men, and the large number of interesting museum articles as well as pictures" that were awaiting some safe place of deposit. "It would," the report continued, "be a place to which the patriotic heart of all Alabamians could turn with pride and delight." It would not only increase the "sense of local importance and State pride, but would also engender a higher degree of respect on the part of sister commonwealths."[11]

The report was well received by the state's newspapers and generated quite an enthusiastic public response. The legislature lost no time in responding to Owen's wishes, and a law of February 27, 1901, adopted by an almost unanimous vote, established the Alabama Department of Archives and History, with a self-perpetuating board of trustees.[12]

The new board promptly elected Thomas McAdory Owen director of the department. With the governor's consent he set up an office in the Senate cloakroom. Although space was restricted, the location was ideal for publicizing and promoting the work that he was struggling to do. Representative and influential men from every part of the state attended the constitutional convention across the hall during the summer of 1901. As opportunity offered, he invited them into his office, unfolded his plans, and listened to their views. Eager to demonstrate the value of the new department, he responded with alacrity to requests of the delegates for statistical or other information and for books and documents. His law practice was permanently forgotten.[13]

Owen did no more fumbling. He knew what he wanted and how to do it, and all the energy he had was devoted to its accomplishment. The wisdom of his judgments and the soundness of his planning are impressive. For the time, he practically gave up writing, except for items intended to give his new department publicity. Recognizing his own rare talents as a collector and organizer, he told the trustees that there were a hundred historical writers for every good collector—and he was right. Writing and research could wait, but not the preservation of perishable records. He had located hundreds of items, and the job was to bring them in, find more, and induce people to save what was in their hands. In his first six months as director, he wrote over a thousand letters. Although recognizing that old swords, pistols, and portraits might not have much value to a historian, he collected them avidly, for the public could see and understand these things, and he needed public understanding and support. He used the Senate chamber for an art gallery.

Owen was always severely pinched for want of funds. His initial salary was only $1800 per year, and an appropriation of $700 had to cover everything else except office space. John Witherspoon DuBose, an old newspaperman and home-grown historian who used a combination of documents and his own reminiscences as sources, told Owen that he was out of work

Thomas McAdory Owen, Sr.

and would probably continue to be. Husbanding his small resources, Owen put DuBose to work at $25.00 per month, writing, editing, and reading proof, for the *Transactions* of the historical society had to be published.

An important part of Owen's plan for his new department was to secure the preservation of state archives. With his official status now established, he worked earnestly to persuade state officials to turn over to him their non-current records, and he took such county records that he could get. Public and private documentary material, pictures, newspapers, relics, and artifacts poured in to him in great volume. Since his office was cramped and his tenure in it insecure, Owen had to be content with only "constructive" possession of most of the archives. The legislature, seeing his plight, made provision for the new Department of Archives and History to occupy space in the contemplated new wing of the capitol and put him on the state capitol building commission. He emerged with nearly half of the new wing, but his activities were severely hampered until he could move in, in January, 1907. In time, the collections overflowed the new quarters and filled several former dwelling houses nearby.

The Alabama Department of Archives and History was the first official governmental archival organization in the United States. A year after its establishment, Mississippi founded an almost exact copy, and numerous other states followed. Owen's contribution was promptly and widely recognized and acclaimed. He became a man of stature in the American Historical Association. At that organization's annual meeting in December, 1904, Owen presented a paper entitled "State Departments of Archives and History," in which he emphasized the importance of a state organization that looked to the preservation of state archives, as well as the other kinds of records that state historical societies, some state supported, were collecting, preserving, and publishing.[14] Warren Upham of the Minnesota Historical Society defended the record of the state-supported societies and insisted that they were better, at least in some states.[15] He must have been right, for both types of institutions exist today as well as combinations of the two. A committee was appointed to consider the matter and to report the following year.[16] Owen's paper, however, was the feature of the day, and he was named chairman of the newly organized Conference of State and Local Historical Societies.[17] The following year, his name was added to the American Historical Association's Historical Manuscripts Commission, on which he served until 1910.

The problem of securing a practical working relationship and co-operation between the state historical society, or department of archives and history, and other organizations with overlapping objectives was one which troubled Owen and other leaders of state historical enterprises. Owen's solution was a loose affiliation, with the department of archives and history sponsoring and advising the other organizations and receiving annual reports from them. His Alabama trustees endorsed the plan at their 1905 meeting.[18] Its success, however, depended upon close personal contact between Owen and the leaders of the other organizations. He had the right personal qualities for the task, but it must have imposed a tremendous burden on him, for he came to hold the presidency or other office in many another organization—state, regional, and national.

In 1911, Owen joined with Dunbar Rowland of Mississippi to memorialize Congress to concentrate federal archives in a National Archives Building. In time, the federal government carried out this plan, to the lasting benefit of historians.[19]

Since the Alabama Historical Society was little more than an alias for Owen, its work was absorbed by the Alabama Department of Archives and History. Through the years, Owen continued vigorously to promote the activities of his department and to carry out the policies he had already laid down. He sponsored or joined numerous historical and patriotic societies,

Thomas McAdory Owen, Sr.

was instrumental in the founding and activities of the Alabama Library Association and the Alabama Anthropological Society. In 1907, he received the national honor of election to the presidency of the Mississippi Valley Historical Association. He gathered material for a compendious topical and biographical history of his state, which was published posthumously after completion by others.[20] It remains a useful work of reference. Owen's death occurred in 1920, in his fifty-fourth year.

Owen's home and his fine personal collections were destroyed by fire in 1906. By that time, his truly great work had been accomplished. Isolated by a lack of professional training from the main currents of historical scholarship, he could not enjoy the full intellectual fellowship of the new generation of southern scholars. Such is often the fate of the really great pioneer developer. Yet his work was probably less ephemeral than theirs—he had saved the past. He was self-trained as an archivist and never fully mastered archival organization, arrangement, classification or cataloging. His devoted and underpaid assistants, too, were home-trained. "Nevertheless," R. D. W. Connor reminisced long afterward, "my visit to him was one of the most profitable experiences of my life. It was not what he had done, nor what he said that dwells with me today: it was what he was. He was energy, he was enthusiasm, he was courage, he was vision, he was faith, he was inspiration, and when I reluctantly bade him good-bye I knew in my heart that some day he would build . . . in Montgomery one of the great archival institutions of the country."[21]

SOURCES AND NOTES

The Owen Papers, located in the Alabama State Department of Archives and History, the Official Records of the Alabama State Department of Archives and History, and the publications of the American Historical Association are the principal sources.

1. Owen to Z. F. Smith, March 13, 1893, Letterbook of Thomas McAdory Owen, 1889-93, business and personal (MS in Owen Papers, Alabama Department of Archives and History, Montgomery, Ala.), p. 289.

2. R. D. W. Connor, "Dedication of the Archival Section of the World War Memorial Building," *American Archivist*, IV (Apr., 1941), 78.

3. C. L. Patton to Owen, Aug. 27, 1896 (MS in Owen Papers).

4. Owen to William Richardson, Jan. 25, 1897, Letterbook of Thomas McAdory Owen, 1888-97, private (MS in Owen papers), p. 439.

5. Owen to W. S. Thorington, Feb. 17, 1897, *ibid.*, p. 446.

6. Thomas McAdory Owen, ed., *Report of the Alabama History Commission to the Governor of Alabama* (Montgomery, Ala., 1901), pp. 5-6.

7. Thomas McAdory Owen, ed., *Transactions of the Alabama Historical Society*, Vol. II, 1897-98 (Tuscaloosa, Ala., 1898), pp. 11-13.

8. *Ibid.*, Vol. III, 1898-99 (Tuscaloosa, Ala., 1899), pp. 17-21. The society's total output in its first forty-eight years had been seven pamphlets and twenty-nine issues of a publication called the *Alabama Historical Reporter*.

9. Act approved on December 10, 1898, in Owen, ed., *Report of the Alabama History Commission*, p. 8.

10. Owen, ed., *Transactions*, Vol. IV, 1899-1903 (Montgomery, Ala., 1904), pp. 34-37, 249.

11. Owen, ed., *Report of the Alabama History Commission*, pp. 37-38.

12. This act, which was widely studied as a basis for the organization of similar agencies in other states, appears in full in American Historical Association, *Annual Report*, 1904, Vol. I (Washington, D.C. 1905), pp. 254-57.

13. "Minutes and Reports: 1901-1906," minutes of the Board of Trustees of the Alabama Department of Archives and History (MS in director's office, Alabama Department of Archives and History, Montgomery, Ala.), annual report of the director, Sept. 30, 1901.

14. The paper appears in American Historical Association, *Annual Report*, 1904, Vol. I, pp. 235-57. An elaborate report on "Alabama Archives," by Owen, is in the same volume on pp. 487-553.

15. American Historical Association, *Annual Report*, 1904, Vol. I, pp. 222-24.

16. For the committee's report see *ibid.*, 1905, Vol. I (Washington, 1906), pp. 251-325.

17. *Ibid.*, 1904, Vol. I, p. 233.

18. *Ibid.*, 1905, Vol. I, pp. 177-78.

19. *Ibid.*, 1911, Vol. I, pp. 324-25.

20. Thomas McAdory Owen, *History of Alabama and Dictionary of Alabama Biography* (4 vols.; Chicago, 1921).

21. Connor, "Dedication of the Archival Section...," *American Archivist*, p. 82. Quoted in Wendell H. Stephenson, "Some Pioneer Alabama Historians: III. Thomas M. Owen," *Alabama Review*, II (Jan., 1949), 55n.

Robert Digges Wimberly Connor

by Hugh T. Lefler

~~~~~~

In October, 1964, the North Carolina Department of Archives and History received the first Distinguished Service Award ever given by the Society of American Archivists. This award was in recognition of "outstanding service to the American people and for exemplary contributions to the archival profession." The outgoing president of the archivists' society noted in the presentation ceremony that North Carolina had long pioneered in developing an archives program. He observed that the man who first developed that program, R. D. W. Connor, was named by President Franklin D. Roosevelt as the first Archivist of the United States and that Connor was one of three North Carolinians who had been president of the society.

Robert Digges Wimberly Connor was born in Wilson, North Carolina, September 26, 1878, the son of Henry Groves and Kate Whitfield Connor. His father served with distinction as a superior court judge, as associate justice of the state Supreme Court, and, from 1909 until his death in 1924, as a federal district court judge.

Young Rob Connor received his formal education in the public schools of his home town and at the University of North Carolina, where he graduated in 1899. In his senior year, he set something of a record by serving as editor-in-chief of all three student publications: the newspaper, the literary magazine, and the yearbook.

The three greatest influences in Connor's life were his father, the University of North Carolina, and his beloved wife, the former Sadie Hanes of Mocksville, North Carolina, whom he married in 1902. In one of his most important books, published in 1919,[1] Connor wrote: "I dedicate this book to my father, Henry Groves Connor, because it was he who first aroused my interest in the history of North Carolina; because by his own life, character and public service he has added dignity and honor to the annals of the State; and because in himself he personifies that reverence for the laws and institutions of democracy, that love of justice, and that faith in the common man which I believe to be characteristic of the people of this Commonwealth."

Connor had hoped to go to the Johns Hopkins graduate school, but he had no money and his father made a small salary and had a large family to educate. So he taught for two years in the public schools of Winston, served for one year as school superintendent in Oxford, and one year as principal of the Wilmington High School. In 1904, he accepted a position as secretary of the State Educational Commission, in the administration of North Carolina's "Educational Governor," Charles B. Aycock.

In this newly created office, Connor became active in the crusade for public education. In numerous letters to educational and political leaders, in speeches, and in newspaper articles, he pleaded with the people of the state to work for better school buildings, higher pay for teachers, improved library facilities, and, above all, for local school taxes to achieve these objectives. He said that he was tired of the word "sacrifice" as applied to school teachers. He could "see no more reason why school teachers should be called upon to sacrifice themselves than any other profession. . . ." He was "in favor of less eulogy and more salary."

In 1903, the North Carolina General Assembly, at the re-

Robert Digges Wimberly Connor

quest of the State Literary and Historical Association, established a State Historical Commission. This new agency was authorized to collect valuable documents pertaining to the history of the state. The commission was to consist of not more than five members and could not spend more than $500 annually for its work. At the commission's first meeting, R. D. W. Connor was chosen secretary.

The commission did not meet again for two years. In fact, it accomplished little until the revision of the original law in 1907.[2] Meanwhile, Connor was active trying to promote interest in the collection and preservation of historical records. The earliest and one of the best statements he ever made on this theme was contained in his address to the State Literary and Historical Association, November 15, 1906. In this paper, printed in pamphlet form and widely circulated, he presented his views on history and his ideas of the importance of historical records. Like others before him, he stressed the importance of collecting, copying, editing, and publishing historical sources before they were lost through carelessness, indifference, or ignorance. Much had already been lost, but much remained in "dark corners, and dusty archives, in pigeon holes, vaults, desks, attics, and cellars" which would readily come to a state-owned safe place for preservation and publication.

Largely through the efforts of Connor and a few other people, the legislature of 1907 revised the original act creating the historical commission. Provision was made for a full-time, salaried secretary, the annual appropriation was increased to $5,000, and the powers and functions of the commission were greatly enlarged. The chief duties of the commission were:

(1) To have collected from the files of old newspapers, court records, church records, private collections, and elsewhere, data pertaining to the history of North Carolina and the territory included therein from the earliest times.

(2) To have such material edited, published as other state printing, and distributed under the direction of the Commission.

(3) To care for the proper marking and preservation of battlefields, houses, and other historic shrines.

(4) To diffuse knowledge with regard to the history and resources of North Carolina.

(5) To encourage the study of the history of North Carolina in the schools, and to stimulate historical investigation among the people of the state.

Connor was re-appointed secretary. He filled that position until 1921, establishing the commission upon a firm foundation and formulating the basic policies that have been followed ever since. Had it not been for his outstanding work in the development of the archival program in North Carolina, it is unlikely that he would have been chosen first Archivist of the United States.

Soon after taking over the secretaryship on a full-time basis, Connor began a vigorous campaign to get people to turn over their valuable documents to the commission. He made this appeal in letters, in speeches, in newspapers, and in brochures. He wrote: "Do you own letters or other documents of historical value? Let the Commission have them and make them accessible to students. Do you know the whereabouts of such documents? Lend the Commission your assistance in procuring them. If the owners of such documents do not wish to part with them permanently, let them be placed with the Commission as a loan, and let the Commission have copies made. . . . All expenses connected with such work will be met by the Commission."

The results of this appeal were most gratifying. In 1921, when he resigned his secretaryship to accept a Kenan Professorship of History at the University of North Carolina, he summarized the work of the historical commission since its establishment.[3] Among other things it

> had saved from destruction, classified and filed many thousands of letters and other documents of the Executive and Legislative Departments from colonial times to the present. It had made an extensive collection, numbering more than 100,000 pieces of material bearing on North Carolina's part in the World War. It had secured for the State more than a score of large private collections numbering many thousands of valuable manuscripts, and several small collections. It had published eighteen books and twenty-seven bulletins. . . . It had maintained the Hall of History, which, with its 12,000 objects was one of the most extensive historical museums in America. . . . It had assisted a large number of students in their historical investigations, and had encouraged in many ways the study of state history in the public schools.

In his letter of resignation,[4] Connor, never a boastful man, said: "I have seen the Commission grow from nothing but an idea and a hope to its present position of importance and influence among its kind in the United States, and I reflect with a great deal of satisfaction that I have had some part in forwarding its development. I feel strongly, however, that the Commission is just emerging from its pioneer period and that its chief work lies before it."

From 1907 to his death forty-three years later, Connor was engaged in historical work as archivist, teacher, and author. As a historian, he demonstrated the instincts of an archivist, and as an archivist he remained a historian. Above everything else, he wished to see the history of his native state presented fairly and fully. To achieve this objective, he realized the need for more monographic studies, better general histories for adults, and more accurate and more interesting history books for the public schools. He took the lead himself in all three of these areas of historical investigation and writing. Among his outstanding books published while he was secretary of the North Carolina Historical Commission were: *Cornelius Harnett: An Essay in North Carolina History* (1909); *Ante-Bellum Builders of North Carolina* (1914); *Revolutionary Leaders of North Carolina* (1916); *Race Elements in the White Population of North Carolina* (1920); and *History of North Carolina: The Colonial and Revolutionary Periods* (1919). His *Makers of North Carolina History* (1911), for many years a basic public-school textbook, is one of the most accurate and interesting books ever published about North Carolina leaders.

Connor taught history and government at his *alma mater* from the fall of 1921 to October, 1934, when he became the first Archivist of the United States. At the university, he was regarded as a superior teacher, with students repeatedly voting him one of their favorite professors. Careful preparation of lectures, systematic organization of materials, clarity and wit in presentation were characteristic of his teaching.

He continued to write books and articles. Outstanding contributions are his two-volume *North Carolina: Rebuilding an Ancient Commonwealth* (1929), and an article entitled "The Rehabilitation of a Rural Commonwealth," published in the *American Historical Review* in October, 1930.

On June 19, 1934, President Franklin D. Roosevelt signed into law the bill creating the National Archives. Even before the law was enacted, J. Franklin Jameson, Conyers Read, and several other distinguished historians took steps "to circumvent the spoilsmen." On May 28, Jameson wrote Read:

> The prospect of getting what we want would be [enhanced] by selecting a Democrat. Though I have carefully avoided naming a candidate, I have for some time been thinking . . . that the best name to propose would be that of R. D. W. Connor. . . . Connor is a man of affairs, who

knows how to deal with politicians. He is, and makes the impression of being, a man of power. He did a fine job in the organizing of the North Carolina Historical Commission and pushed its affairs forward with energy, skill and tact. . . . I think he has the necessary backbone to resist the pressure of office seekers and their senators and representatives, but would not do it unpleasantly. And, as I have intimated, a Southern Democrat would go through the Senate more easily than anybody else.[5]

On October 3, Connor was called to the White House for a conference with the President. The following quotation is Connor's account of this meeting, as recorded in the first of the six-volume "Journal" (unpublished) which he kept during his seven years at the Archives.[6]

After a few pleasantries, the President amazed me by saying: "Mr. Connor, you once did me a valuable service. When I was Assistant Secretary of the Navy, largely through my efforts, Congress appropriated $50,000 to be used by the Secretary of War and Secretary of the Navy to collect from the several states the military and naval records of the American Revolution. Because of my special interest in the project, the job of supervising it for both departments was turned over to me. The appropriation was not enough to cover all of the states, so I concentrated on three of them—Massachusetts, Virginia, and North Carolina. I couldn't locate any North Carolina records in the archives of the Department; but you found them for me in Raleigh and had photostats of them made for me. . . .

"The man I am going to appoint must have two qualifications—he must be a good Democrat and he must have the endorsement of *all* the historians of the country.' To this, I replied: "I can meet the first requirement, Mr. President, but I am not at all sure as to the second."

"Well," he replied, "I am, and I am going to appoint you." [The Executive Committee of the American Historical Association and J. Franklin Jameson had endorsed Connor for the position, see above, p. 92.]

In discussing the kind of documents that should be transferred to the archives building, the President said:

The papers of the President ought to be deposited there. Those in the Library of Congress ought to be transferred to the Archives Building. My own papers, I think, have some historical value; I want them deposited there. Then there is a vast accumulation of dead or inactive records in the various departments which should be transferred there at once—at least as soon as the building is ready.....

McIntyre [Roosevelt's secretary]...interrupted to say, "Excuse the interruption, Mr. President, but Sol Bloom [Democratic Representative of New York and the man who introduced the Archives Bill in Congress] is here to see you about that very matter. He is opposed to putting those files in the Archives Building and says he can get from Congress an appropriation of $2,500,000—or whatever may be necessary—for building a Hall of Records in which to house those dead files, but he protests against turning the Archives Building into a warehouse for a lot of worthless papers.

This led the President to say that he was inclined to agree with Bloom's point of view. The Archives Building was intended to house only valuable historic documents, such as the Declaration of Independence, the Constitution, treaties, Presidential Proclamations, etc. Ordinary office files, correspondence, memoranda, etc. should be deposited in a Hall of Records. What did I think of the idea?

I didn't think much of it and said so, pointing out that what he called "ordinary office files" were in fact among the most important historical sources the Government had; that

Robert Digges Wimberly Connor

they revealed factors, influences, negotiations behind the production of his so-called "valuable historic documents"; and that without one the other would often be unintelligible. Moreover it seemed to me that to talk about another archives building—for that is what the proposed hall of records would be—before the National Archives Building was completed and before anybody had made a study of the Government's needs was premature. He admitted the force of the statement and bringing the conference to a close said: "After you get under way, you must come up and spend the evening with me; there are many things about the Archives I want to talk over with you."[7]

The Hall of Records was never built, though Connor had to talk Secretary of the Interior Harold Ickes out of the idea.

Even before Connor was sworn into his new office, he encountered what he later said were two of his five greatest problems as national archivist: (1) determining the meaning of the word "archives" and (2) patronage—the political pressure for jobs. The other three problems were: transfer of the War Department Records to the National Archives; transfer of the State Department Records, and the alleged controversy regarding a proposal to transfer the Declaration of Independence and the Constitution from the Library of Congress to the National Archives. It should be said here that Connor solved all five of these problems ably and diplomatically.

On October 11, 1934, newspapers announced, "The President yesterday named Professor R. D. W. Connor 'Archivist of the United States' but frankly admitted he was not even sure how to pronounce 'Archivist.'" One newspaper carried a picture of Connor with the headline: "He's U.S. Archivist" and had an explanatory note: "No, dear children, an archivist is not a radical. He is one who preserves historical documents." Connor said that this "enlightening definition" saved him "from investigation by the American Legion."

The newspapers, and perhaps most people who had thought at all about the meaning of the word "archives," had the idea that only rare, unique—or what they chose to call "historic documents"—were covered by the term. The Pittsburgh *Post Gazette* of October 8, 1934, said: "Congress intended the Archives Building for the important state papers and historic documents of the Republic, things like the original Constitution, for example. All this new money for stacks ($3,600,000 P.W.A. Funds) has led to the belief that it is the intent of the bureaucrats to load the costly structure with cart loads of dry-as-dust departmental papers, the usual trash that is wrapped up in customary red tape."

Connor pointed out the absurdity of erecting a $12,000,000 building, containing storage space for a million cubic feet of records, for the sole purpose of housing the Declaration of Independence, the Constitution, some two or three hundred treaties, and a few dozen other so-called "important state papers and historic documents."

He said that this definition of archives was quite as absurd and far less amusing than the one given by his Negro servant, Henry, who had gone to Washington with him from Chapel Hill. At a "tea party" given by the Connors, December 29, 1934,

> The guests were put in good humor immediately upon arrival by finding that the "tea" for which they had so reluctantly come, was in reality a delicious and somewhat subtle planter's punch. The party, therefore, got off to a good start and went merrily along for two or three hours. Henry, my aforementioned servant, circulated among the guests busily distributing canapés of anchovies and, incidentally, hugely enjoying his first Washington party. Among our guests was a former colleague and near neighbor of mine at Chapel

Robert Digges Wimberly Connor

Hill who had known Henry for several years. With two or three glasses of punch safely stored under his shirt and another in his hand, and a happy frame of mind and at peace with the world, he approached Henry and, reaching for an anchovy, asked facetiously, "Henry, what are these things?" In a flash came the response: "Deed, perfesser, ah don't eggsactly know, but ah thinks dey's archives."[8]

Connor confided to his journal that the concept of "archives" as embracing only "important state papers and historic documents was so strongly lodged in the skulls of the newspaper writers that it led them into scribbling a great deal of nonsense on the subject."

Although some newspapers and a few congressmen kept complaining about the "trash" that was being deposited in the archives, these charges eventually subsided. Within a short time, executive departments, independent governmental agencies, United States courts, and "even the United States Senate" began to request Connor to transfer their inactive records to the National Archives Building. According to Connor, "Even the press finally got a glimmer of light as to what it was all about. Reporters began to handle 'archive news' seriously, editorial writers began to take note of our annual reports; special writers began to find in our activities a fruitful source of feature stories for magazines and Sunday papers."[9] At long last, the National Archives had come to be recognized as an important governmental agency.

Connor's second major problem, that of patronage, was not so easily solved. He wrote:

> Having studied and taught history and government most of my adult life, and having had some experience in government service in North Carolina, perhaps I ought to have realized what I was up against. But I didn't. Conditions in the country accentuated the difficulties of the problem. Every-

where people were tramping the streets looking for jobs. Whenever a new government agency was established thousands suddenly discovered that all their lives they had been preparing themselves for the very activities the new agency was to perform. Now trained archivists sprang up in every nook and corner of the country.[10]

The National Archives was able to recruit its staff with exceptionally well-trained people, principally because many excellent scholars coming out of graduate schools were unable to obtain teaching jobs. Despite this situation, which was a fortunate one for Connor, he still had to contend with politicians who insisted on getting their friends jobs. But in 1937, Congress removed the National Archives from the list of "patronage agencies" and placed it under civil service. Connor happily recorded in his journal: "This action brought welcome release from the pressure of patronage brokers and to that extent was a forward step."

As Archivist of the United States, Connor played an important role in the establishment of the Franklin Delano Roosevelt Library at Hyde Park. Early in January, 1938, the President wrote Connor a lengthy memorandum outlining his plans for setting up "for the first time in this country what might be called a source material collection relating to a specific period of history." Roosevelt said that since 1910 he had

> carefully preserved all of my correspondence, public papers, pamphlets, books, etc.... and copies of practically all outgoing material.
>
> Because these papers relate to so many periods and activities which are not connected with my services in the Federal Government, I do not wish to break them up, leaving a portion of them to the National Archives and dividing the rest between the State of New York Archives, the New York State Historical Society, the Dutchess County Historical

Society, the Harvard College Library, the Naval Records Office, etc.

In other words, it is my desire that they be kept as a whole and intact in their original condition, available to scholars of the future in one definite locality. I have carefully considered the choice of locality and for many reasons have decided that it would be best that they remain permanently on the grounds of my home at Hyde Park, Dutchess County, New York....

It is, therefore, my thought that funds can be raised for the erection of a separate, modern, fireproof building to be built near my family's house at Hyde Park, so designed that it would hold all of my own collections, and also such other source materials relating to this period in our history as might be donated to the collection in future by other members of the present Administration (and my administration in Albany)....[11]

A postscript to the memorandum read: "All of this has the approval and consent of my Mother who owns the property during her lifetime."

On January 5, 1937, the President had a conference with Connor and Waldo G. Leland, and agreements were reached concerning such details as the type of filing equipment to be used and the design and use of the exhibition room. It was also agreed that the President's papers then in the White House and Mrs. Roosevelt's papers should be deposited in the new library. Members of the Roosevelt Cabinet were to be urged to place their papers there. Two weeks later, Connor and Leland met with Frank G. Walker to work out financial plans for the library. Walker reported that the building would cost not more than $325,000, and he read a list of persons who had agreed to underwrite the project to the extent of $450,000.

Connor made several trips to Hyde Park while work on the

library building was in progress to discuss with the President a number of problems relating to the library. One of these problems was the choice of a librarian. Roosevelt seemed inclined to appoint Harry Hopkins—a choice that Connor did not approve. The man who was finally appointed, Clifford K. Shipman, had been recommended by Connor and had been a member of the archives staff in Washington.

The Franklin D. Roosevelt Library was dedicated on June 30, 1941, with Connor speaking at the ceremony. But his main interest at this time was in returning to Chapel Hill to accept the newly established Craige Professorship of Jurisprudence and History, a chair that he held until retirement in 1949. He had always loved Chapel Hill; he tolerated Washington. In his own words, he left "the world's greatest bughouse" to return to "the world's greatest intellectual center."

Connor simply picked up where he had left off seven years before. He taught classes in state history and state government. He continued his interest in research and writing. During the last five years of his life, he was hard at work compiling and editing a documentary history of his alma mater. Death came on February 25, 1950, before this job was done, but two of his colleagues edited and saw through to publication a two-volume *Documentary History of the University of North Carolina, 1776-1799*. This was published by the University of North Carolina Press, on whose Board of Governors Connor had served for many years.

SOURCES AND NOTES

The major sources for this essay are: (1) R. D. W. Connor Collection, in the Southern Historical Collection, University of North Carolina Library at Chapel Hill, a large collection that includes hundreds of letters to and from Connor and a six-volume typed, but unpublished, "Journal" kept by him during the seven years he served as archivist of the United States; (2) A 12,000-word unpublished address on R. D. W. Connor, delivered by the author of this essay as his Presidential Address to the Historical Society of North Carolina, November 14, 1958. (3) Various newspapers, too numerous to list.

1. R. D. W. Connor, *History of North Carolina: The Colonial and Revolutionary Periods, 1584-1783* (Chicago and New York, 1919).
2. *Public Laws of North Carolina, 1907*, Ch. 714.
3. *Report of the North Carolina Historical Commission to Governor Cameron Morrison* (Raleigh, 1921).
4. R. D. W. Connor to J. Bryan Grimes, Chairman of the North Carolina Historical Commission, Connor Papers, Southern Historical Collection, University of North Carolina Library at Chapel Hill.
5. Copied in "Journal" of R. D. W. Connor, Vol. I, p. 9, Southern Historical Collection, University of North Carolina Library at Chapel Hill.
6. *Ibid.*, I, pp. 132-34.
7. *Ibid.*, I, pp. 135-38.
8. *Ibid.*, II, pp. 5-6.
9. *Ibid.*, VI, p. 25.
10. *Ibid.*, VI, pp. 34-35.
11. *Ibid.*, II, pp. 2-4.

III. The Historical Museum

George Brown Goode

by G. Carroll Lindsay

Samuel Langley once said of G. Brown Goode, "He interested himself in such varied work that it seemed incomprehensible that one man could accomplish so much in a single life." Langley's tribute is a valid epitaph to a remarkable nineteenth-century figure whose virtuosity was scarcely exceeded by that of Langley himself. In a lifetime of only forty-five years, G. Brown Goode established careers in science, history, genealogy,[1] public administration, and museology. Between 1869 and 1896, 197 articles, monographs, and books were published under his name alone; 152 more by Goode and joint authors; 19 papers and books appeared in print under his editorship, including one work of 7 volumes totaling 3,931 pages; and 16 of the *Annual Reports* of the United States National Museum were prepared under his personal direction. A noted ichthyologist, he was to exercise a major impact on the historical museum.

George Brown Goode was born in Cincinnati, Ohio, in 1851. His mother died eighteen months later, and he was reared by a stepmother, Sally Ann Jackson, whom his father married in 1855. A stepsister, born in 1856, lived less than two years. Of his childhood, Goode records only that he was prepared for college by private tutors in Amenia, New York. This somewhat cryptic statement, coupled with the fact that his father retired from business in 1857, when Goode was six years old, indicates that as an only-surviving child he grew up in a family environment of singularly close personal relationships between child and parents. When he entered Wesleyan University in 1866 for an undistinguished undergraduate career, his parents moved with him to Middletown, Connecticut, and remained there until Goode graduated in 1870.

That fall, Goode began his postgraduate work at Harvard under Louis Agassiz, who was also a member of the Board of Regents of the Smithsonian Institution.[2] A year later (1871), he returned to Middletown as the curator of the natural history collections at Wesleyan University. These collections were housed in the new Orange Judd Hall, the gift to Wesleyan of the agriculturalist and editor for whom it was named, and whose daughter Goode later (1877) married. Goode's first known contact with the Smithsonian dates from 1871 when he wrote to the Institution's first secretary, Joseph Henry, requesting duplicate specimens from the Smithsonian's collections for the new Wesleyan museum and informing Henry of the recent discovery of artifacts from an Indian grave in the vicinity of Middletown.

In 1872, Goode met Spencer F. Baird, then Henry's chief assistant and later secretary of the Smithsonian. Their brief summer encounter in Eastport, Maine, resulted in an immediate personal friendship. Before the year was ended, Sally Goode called on the Bairds, ostensibly to inquire of the potential for her stepson's career in association with the dynamic Baird, but more probably to assess for herself and her husband the character of the man young Goode proposed to take as his mentor. The following year, G. Brown Goode, then twenty-two years old, went to Washington as an assistant curator at the Smithsonian. As did Joseph Henry and many of the scientists who assisted him, Goode not only worked but resided—until his marriage—in the turreted sandstone castle designed twenty-five years earlier by

George Brown Goode

James Renwick as the Smithsonian's headquarters. Later (1887), he built a modest house near the National Zoological Park, where he and his wife, and later one daughter and three sons, were disturbed in their comparative isolation only, as he wrote, "by the caw of the crow and the singing of the locust."

Goode joined the Smithsonian's museum staff—then thirteen strong—as the Institution's policy toward its museum functions was undergoing quiet reappraisal. Henry, nearing the end of his lifetime, continued to try to relieve the Institution of what he regarded as the burdensome responsibility for the ever-growing museum collections in the Smithsonian's charge. If Goode was at this time aware of the quiet conflict between Baird, who saw the collections as a great opportunity for research, and Henry, who regarded the 200,000 specimens as a drain on the Institution's meager financial resources, he has left no record of his own views in the gentle but momentous struggle. Baird, succeeding Henry (1878), was to triumph, with Goode, increasingly important and influential as a museologist, at his right hand.

Three years after coming to Washington, Goode found an unusual opportunity to prove his capacity as a museum administrator. As Baird's chief aide, he was, in effect, in charge of the Smithsonian exhibits at the Centennial Exposition held in Philadelphia's Fairmount Park in the summer of 1876. He supervised the preparation of the exhibit in Washington, its transportation to Philadelphia, and its installation at the exposition. Though his previous experience was limited to work in ichthyology, he carried out his broad Centennial responsibilities with an efficiency that attracted wide attention. After months of the most demanding physical and mental exertion, he returned, an invalid, to Washington.

This marked a turning point in his career. Though he recovered rapidly, he suffered for the rest of his life from what in the late nineteenth century was called "poor health." Langley commented on Goode's "ill health and suffering, his overwrought nervous system and his occasional severe mental depression." A reporter for the Chicago News (October 1, 1891) described him as, "a slender, dark complexioned man of unassuming manner, and wear[ing] a full beard. He is nervous in his actions and smokes cigarettes continually, and does not cease even to converse." Despite the visible nervous tension, Goode unfailingly impressed associates with his highly developed moral and ethical character and unusual sensitivity to the feelings of both his colleagues and his subordinates.

Mark Twain's description of the Smithsonian as "that mildewed fossil," seems hardly in accord with the activities of the Institution reflected in Goode's seethingly energetic career. Hardly had he recovered from the effects of the Centennial Exposition when he was plunged into the building of a new museum. At the conclusion of the Fairmount Park extravaganza in the fall of 1876, some seventy freight carloads of museum material from Philadelphia were shipped to Washington. The Smithsonian was to become the repository of a major portion of the world-wide industrial art exhibits that had attracted some four million visitors. The Institution's acquisition of this vast international representation of nineteenth-century industrial and technological accomplishment was to turn the attention of the entire organization, and especially the facile mind of G. Brown Goode, in an entirely new direction. From the founding of the Smithsonian in 1846 to the Centennial of thirty years later, the work of Henry, Baird, and their associates had been concentrated almost exclusively on the natural and physical sciences. History and technology had remained distinctly secondary interests.

The Centennial collections opened a new vista for the Smithsonian, and of its small staff, Goode was best prepared to accommodate not only the established interest in natural history but also the host of new fields he categorized as "arts and industries." He assumed the leading role in the Smithsonian's assimilation of the new collections.

The red sandstone castle on The Mall was already overflowing with zoological, geological, botanical, and anthropological specimens. Additional museum space was essential. Joseph Henry died in 1878 while the vast new collections remained temporarily stored in wooden shacks on The Mall and in the local armory. The new secretary, Spencer Baird, acted at once and quickly received from a sympathetic Congress an appropriation of $250,000 to erect a suitable building to house the enormous centennial windfall of machinery, ceramics, glass, leather goods, woodenwares, metalwork, graphic arts, sculpture, decorative art, and a host of additional objects and specimens.

Planning and supervising construction of the Smithsonian's red brick Arts and Industries Building—designed by the Washington architectural firm of Claus and Schultz—was a major responsibility of Goode's, but simultaneously he was spending numberless ten- and twelve-hour days superintending the preparation of the first Smithsonian display to be seen outside the United States. His work was one of the major attractions of the Berlin International Fisheries Exposition of 1880. Three letterpress books, totaling some six hundred pages, testify to the administrative energy Goode devoted to this undertaking. Thereafter, he was, with effectiveness and dry humor, to assemble and supervise the Smithsonian's exhibits at the London Fisheries Exposition (1883); the Louisville, Kentucky, Exposition (1884); and the New Orleans Exposition (1885). Later still came Paris, Cincinnati, Atlanta, Chicago, and Madrid where he served as United States commissioner general.

Upon his return from Berlin in the late summer of 1880, he set about the installation of the exhibits in the new museum, and in 1881, Baird appointed him assistant director of the United States National Museum. Baird himself retained the title of director as well as secretary of the Smithsonian Institution until his death in 1887.

In this new position Goode, October 1, 1881, issued *Circular Number One of the United States National Museum*. This fifty-eight page document set forth in minute detail the philosophy for the operation of the museum and the functions of its staff. Though greatly modified over the succeeding eighty-four years, this pamphlet reflects, even today, the basic organizational structure and functions of the United States National Museum. On page eight of the *Circular No. 1* Goode described the threefold function that the organization continues to perform. So important, and so basic even today, are these functions of the United States National Museum that they are quoted here in full as Goode described them in 1881:

> The Museum by these means fulfills a threefold function:
>
> 1. It is a *Museum of Record,* in which are preserved the material foundations of an enormous amount of scientific knowledge—the types of numerous past investigations. This is especially the case with those materials which have served as a foundation for the reports upon the resources of the United States. Types of investigations made outside of the Museum are also incorporated.
>
> 2. It is a *Museum of Research,* by reason of the policy which aims to make its contents serve as fully as possible as a stimulus to and a foundation for the studies of scientific investigators. Research is necessary in order to identify and group the objects in the most philosophical and instructive relations. Its officers are selected for their ability as investigators, as well as for their trustworthiness and abilities as custodians, and its treasures are open to the use of any honest student.
>
> 3. It is an *Educational Museum* of the broadest type, by reason of its policy of illustrating by specimens every kind

George Brown Goode

of natural object and every manifestation of human thought and activity, by displaying descriptive labels adapted to the popular mind, and by its policy of distributing its publications and its named series of duplicates.

In the four generations since Goode described the fundamentals of the Smithsonian's museum activity, and in so doing set forth the functions of every modern research museum, no similar statement has equaled his in succinctness and completeness. Goode wrote *Circular No. 1* when he was thirty years of age. At that time, he had less than nine years' experience at the Smithsonian. His acquaintance with other museums was limited to travel in the eastern United States and to less than a dozen odd European museums he had visited very briefly during the Berlin Fisheries Exposition in the summer of 1880. The museological literature of the day was almost non-existent. His previous writings, except for the classification work done for the Centennial and the annual reports of the Museum of Wesleyan University, had been almost exclusively devoted to ichthyological taxonomy, a field in which he already occupied a prominent position.

The genesis of his museum philosophy, fully though briefly developed in *Circular No. 1,* cannot be thoroughly traced. That it owed much to Spencer Baird, America's foremost early exponent of the research museum, can hardly be doubted. Though Baird certainly understood and fostered Goode's museum tenets, the older man appears to have lacked Goode's ability to organize his museum philosophy in so orderly and comprehensive a manner. Baird's forte lay in action rather than in meditation. It seems fair to credit Goode with considerably more than the parroting of his mentor's thoughts, though *Circular No. 1* obviously mirrored Baird's attitude toward the function of the research museum. Goode's later writings and career make quite clear, however, that he was much more than Baird's museological Boswell.

The year 1887 brought Goode both achievement and double tragedy. In January, Baird named him assistant secretary in charge of the United States National Museum. In this position, Goode emerged more and more clearly as a figure of major significance in the history of the historical museum. In August, his close friend, mentor, and strong supporter, Baird, died.[8] Baird's passing affected Goode perhaps even more deeply than the loss of his aged father three months later.

To Baird's post as secretary of the Smithsonian, the Regents of the Institution appointed Samuel P. Langley. Both Langley and Goode had been appointed as assistant secretaries on the same date (January 12, 1887). Langley was the older by seventeen years. A former director of the Allegheny Observatory in Pittsburgh, Pennsylvania, he was one of the country's leading astronomers. No record of Goode's personal relationship with Langley survives, except Langley's eulogy of Goode written in 1897. Even this appears to have been ghostwritten by other Smithsonian staff members. Evidently, the relationship between the two men was not at all close, though nothing indicates any serious lack of professional harmony between them. Certain facts, however, hint that each kept the other at a distance. Goode's communications to Langley were addressed "Mr. Secretary." He had invariably written to Baird as "My dear Professor Baird." Langley, though a bachelor, had a high regard for children and personally introduced a small exhibition especially designed for juvenile enjoyment at the Smithsonian. Goode, on several occasions, wrote of his general opposition to child-oriented displays, though the Langley "children's room" never seems to have received his direct criticism. Goode thoroughly enjoyed music, sang, played several instruments, and directed that any musical instrument newly added to the collections be brought immediately to his office for inspection and trial. Langley admitted his complete ignorance of Goode's musical interest when he was asked about it after Goode's death.

The American Historical Association had been established in 1884. Five years later, it was incorporated by act of Congress, reporting to Congress through the secretary of the Smithsonian Institution. Goode immediately joined the Executive Council of the association and remained a member for the rest of his life. He regularly attended the annual conventions, and it was here that he delivered his influential "Museum History and Museums of History" in 1888. On these occasions, he visited and exchanged ideas with J. Franklin Jameson, Thomas M. Owen, Reuben Gold Thwaites, and other figures in the first half of the generation of productive ferment that, in the association, bracketed the turn of the century. Goode's contributions lay in his concept of the historical museum as an instrument of public education. Its collections must illuminate the full range of man's activities. Its exhibits, often synoptic, might better be arranged to illustrate a point or, in the later phrase, tell a story than to exhibit one class of object. Labels, often lengthy, not only identified the objects but made clear the relation among the items exhibited. "I am confident," Goode told the American Historical Association, "that the [history] museum may be made a most potent instrumentality for the promotion of historical studies."

Goode had long pursued a personal interest in American history. Even more important, the Institution, in the 1880's, was becoming the country's leading national historical museum. In 1883, Goode, noting that the "Washington Relics" were on public display at the Smithsonian for the first time since the centennial, suggested that these, as well as other antique domestic furnishings, might one day be displayed in an architectural setting of proper scale and date. He made a determined effort to build a great historical collection for the future by including in his accessions much contemporary social and cultural material.

Keepers of the Past

Barnet Phillips, writer for the New York *Times* in 1882, described his friend Goode's plan for the history collections: "This museum is to enter into every detail of human life, not only of the present but of the past, and is to be the custodian of its future. It will show our great-great-grandchildren how their forefathers dressed, how they lived, cooked and ate their food, how they amused themselves, and 1992 will learn of the toys the children of 1882 played with." Goode's was a sense of living history, a historical sense of the importance of the present to the future. Following Goode's policy, the Smithsonian brought to reality Barnet Phillips' prediction, for exhibited in the new Museum of History and Technology are many of the objects, including toys, collected by G. Brown Goode in the 1880's.

By 1895, his philosophy of museum administration fully matured, he addressed the British Museums Association. The paper, "Principles of Museum Administration," drew compliments from museum directors from London to Tokyo. He ended with these words: "The degree of the Civilization to which any nation, city, or province has attained is best shown by the Character of its public museums and the liberality with which they are maintained."

The constant toil of his voluminous writing, strict attention to the multiplicity of details in the administration of his own museum, and the vast and detailed work involved with the many great expositions he helped to superintend took toll of his slight physique. A lengthy rest in Italy, in 1892, failed adequately to restore his strength. Even while vacationing, he visited every Italian museum within reach and kept a lengthy and detailed journal of his travels and observations. Early in September, 1896, he was stricken with a cold. The bronchitis that constantly troubled him became acute and caused his death on September 6, 1896, at the age of forty-five. He was interred in Oak Hill

Cemetery in Georgetown, D.C., the same burial ground that holds the graves of Joseph Henry and Spencer Baird.

Goode was memorialized as a scientist and as a historian in papers prepared by his distinguished contemporaries in these fields. Samuel Langley's memorial paper accorded Goode recognition for his work as a museum administrator. None of his memorialists, however, perceived the most important of his contributions. Viewed in the perspective of the seventy years since his death, it is clear that as a scientist Goode ranks well below such men as Agassiz, Henry, Baird, Langley, and numerous other great names of nineteenth-century American science. As a historian, in the academic sense, his work cannot compare with that of Moses C. Tyler, Charles K. Adams, Herbert B. Adams, George Bancroft, Albert Bushnell Hart, Frederick J. Turner, or the other great nineteenth-century historians who, in effect, founded the scientific study of history in the United States.

But, as an organizer of museum activity, Goode had no peer and, in this field, displayed to the full his vast and unique genius. Under his direction, the Smithsonian museum collections grew from fewer than 200,000 items in 1872 to more than 3,000,000 in 1896, and the museum staff increased over the same twenty-four years from thirteen to two hundred. His organizational ability alone would scarcely make a lasting place for him in American intellectual history were it not for the philosophy from which his organizational talent sprang. George Brown Goode, better than any other American of his time, grasped the real significance of the museum in modern life. He realized the contribution, both to academic scholarship and to public education, that the great, broadly based museum of science, history, and art might make. He was the first American to begin to realize the role of the museum in synthesizing the study of science, art, and history. Goode was both the product of the nineteenth-century's attitude toward science, as reflected in the careers of Henry, Baird, and Langley, and the embodiment of the eighteenth-century enlightenment of Franklin and Jefferson. Goode struggled throughout his life to accommodate the diversities of science, history, and art within the framework of his museum philosophy. While Henry Adams boggled at the "multiplicity" and "complexity" of the nineteenth century, Goode dealt with the same problem on a practical working level, incorporating into his educational museum exhibits a theme of continuity and valid relationships between diverse objects, following a pattern unfamiliar either to scientist or historian of the time.

Trained as a scientist, and working with scientists in the nation's leading scientific institution, Goode, in his efforts to find a common bond among history, science, and art, naturally followed a course heavily influenced by the scientific approach. Indeed, so great was the influence of science in Goode's day that even the strictly academic historians of the 1880's and 1890's made valiant efforts to press the study of history into a scientific mold. In preparing catalogues of his museum exhibits and exposition displays, Goode often made tortuous attempts to devise a scientific taxonomy applicable to historical objects. It is a testimony to his intellectual perspicacity that he himself remained unsatisfied with these efforts. Nowhere was this intellectual conflict more apparent than in his display of ethnological materials. Unable to decide whether the correct classification for cultural material was by function or by cultural association, he arranged such items according to a double classification in the halls of his museum. He carefully equipped his exhibit cases with castors and, in a matter of an hour or two, could have the entire display rearranged by either function or cultural association as the need required. However, the triumph of the scientific influence is apparent in the fact that he regarded the functional classification as the "permanent" arrangement, and the cultural one as only temporary.

George Brown Goode

Whatever the shortcomings of his historical display classification may have been, Goode recognized, perhaps better than the academic historians of his time, the practical problems inherent in attempts to fit historical data into scientific taxa. Unreasonable as his approach to the arrangement of historical and cultural objects may appear to the historian or museologist of today, his solution was certainly no more a "scientific" one than the general approach to the study of history undertaken by the leading historians on the faculties of American universities of the day.

In any event, the detailed success or failure of his efforts in displaying historical material is altogether secondary to Goode's brilliance in understanding the importance of history as a legitimate, indeed vital, subject for development by the research museum.

"Chaos," wrote Henry Adams, "was the law of nature. Order was the dream of man." Order was essentially the dream of G. Brown Goode, whether in classifying nature or history. In this, he was truly the intellectual product of the nineteenth century, neither greater nor lesser than his academic contemporaries. But his great gift to the Smithsonian and to the museum world of today was a valid philosophy for the function of the complete research museum, an early and trail-blazing attempt to incorporate into the activity of the research museum not only science but the study of history, and the effort to use both for public education. How history has fared in the museum world over the past seventy years is neither to the fault nor to the credit of G. Brown Goode but the result of how well or how poorly his successors have built upon the foundation he laid.

SOURCES AND NOTES

No thorough biographical study of G. Brown Goode has been published. Shortly after his death numerous brief memorial papers appeared in the journals of various local Washington, D.C., scientific and historical

Keepers of the Past

societies. These, and Goode's more important historical and museological papers, were published in Part II of the *Annual Report* of the U.S. National Museum for 1897 (Washington: Government Printing Office, 1901). The most complete account of Goode's career is an article by Paul H. Oehser in *The Scientific Monthly*, Vol. LXVI, No. 3 (March, 1948), 195-205.

The archives of the Smithsonian Institution contain much of Goode's vast administrative correspondence but almost nothing of a personal nature. Many of his writings were published or reprinted by the Institution, and a complete bibliography of his works appears in the *Annual Report* of the U.S. National Museum for 1897. Some additional information appeared in the local Washington newspapers of the period 1875-96 which carried notices of Goode's activity.

The Smithsonian acquired Goode's large personal library shortly after his death, but these items have been assimilated into the general Smithsonian library collections and are no longer maintained as a unit; no catalog of his library is known. The whereabouts of such personal papers as he may have possessed is unknown if, indeed, such papers even exist.

1. Goode's excursion into genealogy resulted in a masterpiece of its kind, the 526-page *Virginia Cousins,* published in 1887. In the prologue he wrote, "I am sorry that the book is not better and more accurate," but went on to explain, "the time for this work has been stolen from leisure hours."

2. What influence, if any, Agassiz, who died in 1873, may have exerted in obtaining a Smithsonian post for Goode is uncertain.

3. Goode succeeded Baird as the chief of the United States Fish Commission, a post he held only briefly, preferring to give his full attention to museum work, despite the urging of President Cleveland that he remain in the Fish Commission.

Edgar Lee Hewett

by James Taylor Forrest

~~~~~~

Edgar Lee Hewett was largely responsible for the founding of the Museum of New Mexico in Santa Fe—one of the nation's leading museums—and was its director from 1909 until his death in 1946. His interests were varied, his energies abounding, and during his long life, he was in restless pursuit of the tools and the means of forging more reliable implements for teaching and imparting knowledge. Hewett indicates his motivation in his introduction to a book titled *From Cave Dwelling to Mount Olympus:* "Nature and man were the two big factors in a quest that had led me over a considerable part of the continents and the seven seas . . . to know nature I had to get out and see her in a wide world, then come back to get the close-up view in laboratory and museum. To know humanity I had to go among peoples of all kinds in their own environments, see the places where they and their ancients lived and recorded their lives; then settle down to read the observations of other travelers and historians and ethnologists. . . ."

In brief summary, he also taught in rural schools, colleges, and universities; performed research in Italy, Greece, Palestine, Egypt, Mexico, as well as in the United States; was director of American Research for the Archaeological Institute of America;

director of the School of American Archaeology (now the School of American Research); director of exhibits in science and art of the Panama-California Exposition, San Diego, 1911-16; special lecturer at the American School of Oriental Research, Jerusalem and Baghdad, and served with the Yale-Babylonian Expedition in Palestine, Syria, Arabia, and Mesopotamia, 1923.

Hewett went on explorations in Morocco, Algeria, Tunisia, the Sahara, Asia Minor, and the Mediterranean Islands; directed excavation of the ancient Mayan city of Quiriguá, Guatemala; directed numerous excavations among the ancient cliff dwellings and pueblos of Colorado, Utah, Arizona, and New Mexico, where, as well as in California, he also made anthropological expeditions. He directed field classes in Mexico, Guatemala, Peru, Bolivia, and Ecuador; made known and named the cliff dwelling region of Pajarito Plateau, New Mexico; drafted federal laws (passed in 1906) for the preservation of American antiquities and national monuments, and state laws in New Mexico (passed in 1931) for the conservation of scientific resources. He conducted the archaeological survey in 1906 that formed the basis for establishment of Mesa Verde National Park; was a fellow of the American Association for the Advancement of Science; a life member of the Archaeological Institute of America; chairman of state historical service and director of State Child Welfare Service of New Mexico; vice-president of the American Federation of Arts; and a member of the Himalayan Research Institute. He was the author of many books and pamphlets on history, education, and anthropology.

These are the bare bones of a remarkable career. Hewett's life began on a farm in Illinois, in 1865, just at the close of the Civil War. The aftermath of that war, as well as the American pioneer tradition and the westward movement, were part of his time and heritage. The youngest of five children, he led a normal farm childhood. From his mother, born in Kentucky, he heard tales of the wilderness and of her family's move across the frontier to Illinois. His father had gone in his youth, via Panama, to participate in the California gold rush. His grandfather, Colonel Harvey J. Hewett—murdered for his money—had had large holdings in land and stock.

Until he was fourteen, Edgar had little formal schooling. He attended school only three or four months a year—normal at that time in the relatively isolated farm lands of the Midwest. However, he read at home with his mother and, as he put it, developed a "hunger in the head." He liked adventure stories and stories about people and distant places. He devoured Bayard Taylor's *Travels* and the works of John L. Stephens about the Maya ruins, as well as Dickens and Scott.

When the family moved to Hopkins, Missouri, his personal world broadened. To the Hopkins High School, a mile and a half away, he trudged through the Missouri mud and dust. The principal, though not a really learned man, stimulated his desire for knowledge and taught him how to search for and find what he wanted to know.

In his later high school years, Edgar boarded with a family, milking cows and taking care of the horses for his keep. In his senior year, he worked in a drug store for his room and boarded for $1.50 a week. As a high school graduate, he faced the world with $14.35 in his pocket.

At Fairfax, Missouri, after passing the examination for a teacher's certificate, he began his teaching career as a country school teacher at $36.00 a month. During the summer, he attended the four weeks' session of the Teachers' Institute at Tarkio, where, by helping on the teaching staff, he was able to earn enough to pay his expenses. Later, through a chance meeting with one of the professors, he attended the new college at Tarkio, which he was able to enter as a junior and earn his expenses by teaching bookkeeping, commercial law, and related subjects.

At times he was asked to take the classes of the ailing President Marshall and finally was made professor of history and literature at $80.00 a month, double his previous salary. He must already have been showing the personality and strength of character that later made him such an effective executive and teacher. He reported that, at this time—and for most of his life —he went to bed at 2:00 A.M. and awakened at 6:00 A.M.

After about a year as a professor, he was offered an opportunity to read law in the office of a prominent lawyer. He accepted, although he had no intention of becoming a lawyer, because he felt a knowledge of law might be useful. By the time he was prepared to take the bar examination, he returned to Fairfax, Missouri, as principal of schools. He next became superintendent of schools at Florence, Colorado, and on September 16, 1891, married Cora E. Whitford in Denver.

During the long summer vacations when Hewett was not teaching, he and his wife camped out in Colorado and the nearby states, seeing the ruins of prehistoric Indian dwellings and the way of life of the modern Indians, many of whom were descended from the prehistoric tribes. Among the places that he probably saw during this period were Mesa Verde in southwestern Colorado, the great communal structure at Chaco Canyon in northwestern New Mexico, and the various kinds of prehistoric dwellings that honeycomb the volcanic tufa of the Pajarito Plateau, which lies northwest of Santa Fe.

Archaeological work in the Old World had uncovered places described in the Bible or in the works of classical authors. American archaeology, on the other hand, was in the early stages of development. Only a few books or accounts were available regarding the prehistoric Indians on the American continent, and but little had been recorded concerning the culture of the living Indian. With what had been done, Hewett was familiar. He recognized the great opportunities in this field in America and, wanting to make a contribution, did his first field work on the Pajarito Plateau in 1896.

Edgar Lee Hewett

The best-known feature of this plateau, with its traversal canyon, is Bandelier National Monument, with the remains of a tremendous community house, as large as many of our modern apartment houses, fantastic dwellings built against the cliff walls. Winding through the canyon flows a small stream called El Rito de los Frijoles (Little River of the Beans), by which name the area is sometimes known. North, and along Santa Clara Creek, stands Puye, with an abandoned pueblo structure on the mesa top and more ancient cliff dwellings built against the sides of the mesa. Hewett's reports and later writing on this area were influential in at least two unsuccessful efforts by Congress to establish a national park around the Pajarito Cliff cities.

Aware of the need for protecting the Indian antiquities from vandalism and pot-hunters, Hewett helped Congressman J. F. Lacey of Iowa formulate proposals for the protection of these sites. These proposals resulted in a federal law, in 1906, to preserve historic and prehistoric landmarks and scenic wonders for future generations; in turn, this led to passage of similar acts by Arizona, New Mexico, and other states.

In 1903, Hewett decided to make archaeology his major interest and to continue his education at the University of Geneva. He worked there in 1904, but it was not until 1908 that he received his Ph.D. His doctoral thesis, written in acceptable French, concerned *Les Communautes anciennes dans le desert americain*.

During the time he was working on his advanced degree, he was involved in a number of other activities. In January, 1906, he became fellow in American Archaeology, under the Archaeological Institute of America. The institute, organized in 1879 to co-ordinate archaeological activities, had already established schools for research in Palestine, Athens, and Rome.

This fellowship allowed Hewett to study ancient Indian ruins in Mexico. He was also asked by the United States government to make a survey of Mesa Verde to determine whether, under the pending legislation, that area should be made a national park. In addition, he lectured in many cities, including Santa Fe, New Mexico, where he aroused the interest of the people in their limitless archaeological treasures. Hewett urged the building of a good road to the cliff dwellings and the printing of circulars about them and how to reach them. He spoke of the work of the Archaeological Institute and the local work being organized in Colorado, Utah, and California.

As a result of Hewett's work and enthusiasm and the increased interest in American archaeology, the Archaeological Institute, in 1907, established the School of American Archaeology and Hewett was named its director. For two years, field work in co-operation with local archaeological societies was carried on in New Mexico, Colorado, and Utah. The school was not one of classrooms or curriculum but of research. Already Hewett was talking about the value of field museums at the sites of the excavated ruins, which would make the ancient cultures more intelligible to visitors.

The School of American Archaeology was a school without a location, existing only where its director might be. Hewett early thought of Santa Fe as a suitable location for the school, lying as it did in an area rich in prehistoric treasures and, as he put it, mid-way between Panama and Alaska. Santa Fe's historic Palace of the Governors also seemed destined to be a museum and a proper place to house the school. Built by order of the Spanish Crown in 1610, the palace had seen history in the making for three hundred years. Now its days of glory as the center of government were over.

In 1885, the Historical Society of New Mexico had acquired rooms in the east end of the building to house its collections. When the federal government turned the palace over to the Territory of New Mexico in 1898, it presented a real problem for New Mexico, which was well aware of the historic value of the adobe structure yet lacked the money to keep the building in repair.

The palace was offered, in 1901, to the federal government to become a branch of the National Museum, and other proposals were later presented which were not adopted. To produce income, rooms in the palace were rented as private offices. Had not the destinies of Hewett and the palace joined, the venerable building might have gone to complete ruin. However, after conferences with representatives of the Archaeological Institute, the territorial legislature, by act of February 19, 1909, established the Museum of New Mexico in the Palace of the Governors, which also became a seat for the School of American Archaeology. The director of the school was to serve as director of the museum but not receive any salary from state funds.

It was, indeed, a somewhat confused situation that faced Hewett: two museums in one building, with little money and only a small staff to care for a rapidly expanding program in history, archaeology, and, later, art. Another complication, which became more apparent after Hewett's death, was the union of the museum, a state institution, and the school, an independent organization. While Santa Fe and New Mexico tended to think of Hewett as director of the museum, with his chief activities centered there, his view of his task was much broader. As director of the School of American Archaeology, in line with the statements of the Archaeological Institute, Hewett saw his work as covering the culture areas of the entire American continent, directing expeditions of local archaeological societies in their respective fields, and training students in archaeological work.

In 1909, the year the Museum of New Mexico was established, Hewett spent only part of the time in Santa Fe. In early spring, he went to Spain to investigate the Spanish archives relating to America. During that year, he also lectured in innumerable places around the country, made a short visit to Yucatan in November, and, during the summer, personally supervised exca-

Keepers of the Past

vations at Puye and Rito de los Frijoles. The first annual meeting of the Board of Regents of the Museum was held at the Puye excavations, which gave the board a better concept of what was being done and the problems involved.

In the following year, two rooms devoted to materials from the Rito de los Frijoles and Puye were finished in the museum and the museum opened in August. The work had been completed with the help of donations from Frank Springer of Santa Fe, the Woman's Board of Trade, and the Archaeological Society of New Mexico. Dr. Hewett had a great talent for obtaining contributions to aid his work.

The year 1911 began with Hewett, Sylvanus G. Morley, Jesse L. Nusbaum (of the school and the museum), and J. P. Adams (surveyor) in Quiriguá, Guatemala, where excavations were made financially possible by the St. Louis Archaeological Society and the United Fruit Company. Excavations were conducted there for three seasons.

Trouble had meanwhile been brewing between the historical society and the museum. In 1912, the year New Mexico became a state, the matter came to a head. Various bills were introduced in the legislature with regard to the use of the palace. Bills favored by the historical society were passed by the House, but failed of passage by the Senate. In fact, the historical society ended up without its usual appropriation of $500 for maintenance and $500 for acquisition of historical items. The museum, on the other hand, received an appropriation of $5,000 with which it ultimately put the entire building in order. The situation was hardly calculated to improve relations between the two groups.

Indeed, few men as dynamic and aggressive as Edgar Hewett can help making enemies. He was able to accomplish what he did largely through the strength of his personality. He defined his work as destiny: knowing so clearly what you want to do and be that everyone and everything can be enlisted to help.

Edgar Lee Hewett

He made loyal, lasting friends who helped him accomplish what he wanted to do, but he also made enemies. The 1912 difficulty prompted one of the occasions on which his detractors raised a hue and cry against him in the newspapers: "the Museum needed a director who could devote more than a few weeks of the year to the institution . . . one who covered so much ground, geographically speaking, could not be thorough in anything. . . . Hewett manipulated things and people, so that the minority voice of disagreement could not be heard . . . his scientific qualifications were not sufficient. . . ."

Friends leaped to his defense, and others were afraid that antagonism to Hewett might cause withdrawal of the School of American Archaeology from Santa Fe. Hewett maintained public silence and did not voice his thoughts in print. Behind the scenes, wheels were undoubtedly turning. The clamor of the opposition died down, and Hewett continued on his way.

With work on the Palace of the Governors completed, Hewett was already dreaming of larger horizons—of a museum devoted to ethnology and art, as well as archaeology and history. In his annual report of 1912, he first spoke of the need for an additional building to house the museum's ever-increasing collections.

The activities of the museum expanded in other directions as well, as the museum sought to preserve New Mexico's antiquities. As a result, the abandoned Franciscan mission and Indian pueblo of Quarai was deeded to the museum for excavation and preservation. This and other sites, such as Pecos, Abo, and Jemez, later became state monuments. Hewett saw an immediate and future value in these unique centers. In all instances, they represented both the Indian and the Spanish cultures. He began by making careful scientific examination of the remains; checked all available written documents concerning their history and their architecture; restored and reconstructed buildings where feasible; protected the sites from careless destruction; and, finally, established small museums or interpretation centers to serve the interests of curious visitors. Pecos will soon become a federal monument; Abo and Quarai are isolated but have thousands of visitors each year; Jemez built a new visitors' center in 1964 and its stone mission was stabilized. All but Pecos are to be continued as Museum of New Mexico field centers and, eventually, improved along the general pattern developed for Jemez. The work begun by Hewett continues.

With the participation of the New Mexico Archaeological Society, the publication of *El Palacio,* a periodical devoted largely to reports of the activities of the school and museum, was begun. Although form and content have changed from time to time, *El Palacio* is still published by the Museum of New Mexico, and it is still largely devoted to the interests of archaeology and particularly to those of the Archaeological Society of New Mexico though other material is also published.

Artists had been coming to New Mexico in increasing numbers, and exhibits of their paintings were being held in the Palace of the Governors. At San Diego, also, where the director and the staff of the museum and school were busy, the work of many regional artists, including J. H. Sharp, Ernest Blumenschein, Bert Phillips, Irving Couse, Walter Ufer, Oscar Berninghaus, Victor Higgins, was displayed.

Most important, perhaps, Hewett's wish for a new building was quickly fulfilled. The New Mexico legislature, in 1915, provided for the construction in Santa Fe of a replica of the New Mexico Building at the Panama-California Exposition in San Diego. After some difficulties, a suitable site for the building was obtained on the corner across the street from the palace, and the building of what is now the Fine Arts Building commenced.

The year 1917 saw the completion and dedication of the art building. The opening exhibition featured works by such artists as John Sloan, William Glackens, and George Bellows—all of

Edgar Lee Hewett

whom became staunch supporters of the new art interest of the museum. It was the year of the United States' entry into World War I. It also marked the end of the decade since the founding of the School of American Archaeology. To broaden the work of the school and give it legal status to accept endowments, the school was, in 1917, incorporated under the laws of New Mexico, and its name changed to School of American Research. In his annual report of 1918, Hewett summarized the first ten years' work as including research work in the United States, Mexico, and Central America; preparation of students for research work; building the museums of Santa Fe and San Diego (the latter for the Panama-California Exposition); aid in preserving American antiquities; revival of native American arts and drama; stimulation of the Southwest art movement; renaissance of New Mexican architecture; publication of reports and a quarterly magazine; and awakening of wide popular interest in, and better understanding of, native American culture. Hewett's thinking had both changed and broadened.

During the next few years, he spent more time in broadening the activities of the museum, encouraging Indian artists to paint watercolor pictures relating to their culture and ceremonies; stimulating Indian arts and crafts and particularly pottery-making, by showing the craftsmen the ancient pottery and old designs used by their ancestors; and, at the revival of the Santa Fe Fiesta, providing a market where the Indians could sell their wares. (On the portal in front of the Palace of the Governors today the Indians still come to sell their pottery, jewelry, and other handicrafts.) Further excavations were carried on in New Mexico, in co-operation with other institutions, and the beginnings of a field museum at Rito de los Frijoles were made.

Hewett, in 1923, on sabbatical leave, visited archaeological sites in Palestine, Syria, and Mesopotamia, and attended the inauguration of the American School of Oriental Research in Baghdad.

Keepers of the Past

But he was soon back at work in Santa Fe. Excavations and gifts continued to increase the collections of the museum. The library was growing. It was reported that there were books in fifty languages. Hewett's interest in ethnology, the culture of the living Indian, was expanding. He complained of the lack of funds for the purchase of modern Indian materials to supplement the museum's collections—this was to remain one of the museum's most serious problems. Hewett's early interest in the science of man had broadened and become better defined. He thought of history in the Southwest, not as confined to approximately four hundred years of written history, since the coming of the Spanish, but as covering the whole span of man, from prehistoric times to the present. His interest in art was also growing in that direction to cover all the centuries of man's creativity in the Southwest.

Hewett now defined research as including excavation, exhibits in the museum, and publications. He felt that the artists painting in New Mexico were as truly researchers as were the scientists.

With the expansion of the collections, Hewett naturally thought in terms of additional buildings. In 1926, what he envisioned as necessary for the proper growth of the museum included devoting the Palace of the Governors to history (accomplished only in 1964) with the restoration of several rooms to their original state; consigning the Fine Arts Building, as it was, to art; constructing a building for archaeology, another for ethnology, and a library quadrangle with a specially constructed fireproof Hall of Records that would house the New Mexico archives; and building a quadrangle for laboratories and workshops for the preparation of museum material, for printing, and for bookbinding.

He suggested that, to meet the needs of the museum for the next fifty years, the two buildings north of the palace, substantial but unsightly, should be acquired. These buildings were

Edgar Lee Hewett

the armory and the Elks Club. Not only would the acquisition of these buildings by the museum add necessary space, but the architecture around the Plaza would be improved by remodeling these buildings to conform to more traditional Santa Fe style—or better still, they could be torn down, and others built conforming to the architecture of the palace. He realized that the cost of acquiring these buildings would be beyond the means of the state and proposed trying to secure the necessary funds from outside sources.

It was many years before even a portion of Hewett's well-considered plans became accomplished fact. The museum acquired the armory in 1938. This building then became the Hall of Ethnology (Hall of the Modern Indian), devoted to models of Indian dwellings, Indian crafts, and other modern Indian materials. Only in 1963, seventeen years after Dr. Hewett's death, did the museum acquire title to the Elks Club, with funds appropriated by the New Mexico legislature. The Hall of Records became a reality in a way quite different from that contemplated by Hewett. In 1960, the State Records Center, apart from the museum, was established to house and preserve the New Mexico archives, which were then turned over to it by the museum, and to care for the masses of old records of the various agencies of the state. A proper building for the library was earlier and more easily obtained by building a wing onto the northeast end of the palace. This wing, dedicated in January, 1931, houses the collections of the Museum of New Mexico, the Historical Society of New Mexico, and the School of American Research.

Realizing the museum was a state-wide institution, Hewett conceived a program that was termed "decentralization" of the museum's collections. Branch museums already had been installed in Silver City, in Raton, at the University of New Mexico, and at the ruins of Puye. The plan for the expansion of the program proposed that local communities with sufficient interest, and preferably near archaeological sites, should provide a building for a local museum and establish an organization to assume responsibility for its operation. The nucleus of the local collection would be provided by the branch museum, and this would be supplemented by surplus archaeological materials from the state museum, which would also assist in installing the collections in the proper manner and in other ways assist in the local museum's program. This plan has made possible the operation of many small community museums in New Mexico.

In 1930, Hewett's first major work, *Ancient Life in the American Southwest,* was published. He had, of course, published numerous papers before this time and continued to do so afterward. A bibliography of his writings contains more than two hundred items.

The year 1935 marked Hewett's seventieth birthday, and to honor him an anniversary volume was planned by some of his associates and former students. This book, *So Live the Works of Man,* edited by Donald D. Brand and Fred E. Harvey, was published in 1939 by the University of New Mexico Press and covered as wide a range of interests as Hewett's own.

Hewett died on December 31, 1946, in the Presbyterian Hospital in Albuquerque, from which he had continued to administer the affairs of the museum and arrange for his successor: Dr. Sylvanus G. Morley, who had been one of his first three students at the field school of 1907. Hewett, in effect, wished to control certain things from beyond the grave, and perhaps to some extent he did through his vision and the institutions that he built. Certainly, the strength of his character lived on long after his death.

Edgar Lee Hewett was by his own definition, but not by his own admission, an educated man, one who devoted his life to the cause of learning. He often pondered the real meaning of "wisdom," but he never lost faith in man's capacity to learn nor faltered in his belief that all education must be based on the

Edgar Lee Hewett

"knowledge of man...and in an understanding of his nature and destiny." He was an idealist; he wanted perhaps most of all to pass on to the world his ideals of Man.

People who knew him still revere his memory, though some feel that his real contributions were not in the field of science. This may be so because of his reluctance in later years to recognize and accept new advances in the field of archaeology. He was an inspired and inspiring teacher, essentially a teacher in all he said and did. The names of his students who went on to become noted in their fields are legion.

He also built well, and to him the Museum of New Mexico owes a considerable debt. His vision of its future may yet be realized. Even now it is one of the great museums of the nation. Hewett was the architect of one of the Southwest's important educational institutions. The museum remains as one of the few state museums concerned with broad interests in art, history, folk art, and anthropology. Its collections in ethnology and archaeology are considered outstanding; its educational potential, through its collections and libraries, is considerable. Hewett's interest in the Indian and his culture has led to the preservation of fine examples of ancient and modern arts and crafts; the ruins of pueblo and cliff dwellings have been preserved for the public. The Spanish missions, which might otherwise have been lost to the ravages of weather and man, have been stabilized and are a part of the state's historic site program. The growth of interest in these things seems to indicate that what he fought for will now be carefully guarded and maintained.

Hewett's last legacy was to leave with *his* museum his plans for a brighter future and much of his own fortune. He gave property in Santa Fe and funds so that a portion of the work might continue, knowing as he did the ever-present needs of such an institution.

Keepers of the Past

SOURCES

The main sources were the Hewett and other papers and the records of the museum in the Museum of the New Mexico Library. Hewett's published works are also useful, especially *Two Score Years*, 1946; *From Cave Dwelling to Mount Olympus*, 1943; *Man and the State*, 1944; *Campfire and Trail*, 1943; *Man and Culture*, 1944, all published by the University of New Mexico Press. Also helpful are the published papers and reports of the School of American Research, the School of American Archaeology, the Archaeological Institute of America, the Museum of New Mexico, and a paper on Edgar L. Hewett by Julia K. Shishkin, Sante Fe, N.M., 1963.

George Francis Dow

by Charles B. Hosmer, Jr.

If we follow Webster's definition of the word "antiquary" strictly, we will find that an astonishing number of people fit it to some degree. An antiquary is described as "a student of old times through their relics; one who collects or studies antiquities." It would be impossible to have such people today unless a few dedicated individuals in the past had devoted their lives to collecting and studying objects, and George Francis Dow was certainly one of the most notable of all American antiquaries. Unfortunately, the definition of antiquary should perhaps be carried a bit further and end with this statement: "The antiquary is so involved in the study of relics of the past that he rarely mentions his own accomplishments and therefore is frequently pictured as a colorless bookworm." In the case of George Francis Dow, nothing could be further from the truth. He was not the leader of a nationally significant organization, but he was the originator of many ideas that have influenced our times.

George Francis Dow was born in Wakefield, New Hampshire, January 7, 1868, and grew up in Topsfield, Massachusetts, where he attended the public schools. Then at Bryant and Stratton Commercial School in Boston, he prepared for a mercantile career. From 1885 until 1898, he was in the wholesale metal business in Boston, and there is reason to think that he was a success in his work. However, young Dow did not find the hardware business a suitable outlet for his great energy, and he began to turn to the study of local history for his satisfaction. In 1893, he began editing a local paper, the *Topsfield Townsman*, which only lasted a few years. In 1894, he organized the Topsfield Historical Society and conducted its first meetings in his home. His interest in the town led him to arrange tours for people who wanted to learn more about the region around Topsfield. He edited and helped to publish a series entitled *The Historical Collections of the Topsfield Historical Society*.

His reputation in the antiquarian field had spread so widely by 1898 that he was offered the post of secretary of the Essex Institute in Salem, Massachusetts, one of the largest and oldest local historical organizations in the United States. Dow was an ideal choice for the position because he was able to manage the finances of the institute as well as undertake research and publishing ventures. As secretary of the Essex Institute, he was responsible for publishing the *Historical Collections* of that organization, as well as building up the library and museum. Here was the perfect task for an antiquary, and Dow quickly proved to the members of the institute that he was a true collector: "The Secretary is always glad to advise and assist in the disposal of any material which the householder may wish to discard. If the accumulation *seemingly* has no value and is about to be destroyed, please send a postal notification of the fact and we will gladly send for it and by personal inspection separate the grains of wheat and then destroy the chaff. . . ."[1]

Many of the "grains" of historical "wheat" that Dow sought were in manuscript form. He found in the files of the institute several diaries that he believed were vital to an understanding of the history of Salem and Essex County, so he began editing them for the *Historical Collections* of the institute. Dow found old newspapers even more helpful. Almost every day he would spend several hours scanning ("gleaning" as he called it) eighteenth- and nineteenth-century newspapers for advertisements and news items that illustrated everyday life. He was particularly interested in descriptions of household furnishings, table settings, and comments on food. Dow also eagerly sought collections of engravings and photographs for the institute, because he considered them as valuable a source as written material. After the directors of the institute had decided to buy some old pictures depicting Salem in former days, Dow wrote in his report: "We are the builders and the preservers for those who are to come after us."[2]

The word "antiquary" might imply dryness to many people, but the only thing that was dry about Dow was his ever-present humor. His first reports for the Essex Institute were marked by comments on visitors who asked him where the spot was where the witches had been burned (they were hanged); and, one year, five people came to see the original scarlet letter!

George Francis Dow was not an aimless collector, for he firmly believed in the educative mission of the Essex Institute. In 1907, he outlined his own program: "Now if the museum has possessed an educational influence in the past, particularly during the congested conditions of recent years, it is most certain that much more effective work will be possible in the future, for the rearranged collections will illustrate, in an almost unique manner, the every-day life of our forefathers."[3]

He then proceeded to implement his daring suggestion that the life of his "forefathers" could be illustrated. First, he rearranged the exhibit hall of the institute when a new building was added in 1907. The hall included clothes, a variety of utensils, and some fragments of old buildings that had been torn down in the Salem area. The second step in his program was the addition of some "period rooms" that had old woodwork and furnishings put together to resemble a room that had been in use about a century before. The final step in Dow's plan was the most ambitious of all—an outdoor museum in the yard behind the Essex Institute. His program was to make the institute one of the first museums in America to exhibit large numbers of handicrafts, the first to install a number of period rooms, and the first to assemble an outdoor museum.

Dow's inexhaustible store of energy enabled him to carry through this whole ambitious project step by step. After setting up the new exhibitions, he turned to the period rooms. He selected three alcoves along one wall of the large exhibit room and then proceeded to recreate a kitchen of 1750, a bedroom of 1800, and a parlor of 1800. These little rooms were three-sided, for the fourth side was a glass partition that permitted the visitor to inspect the room without actually entering. Most of the wood finish in these alcoves came from buildings that had been dismantled, and in the parlor Dow designed a room to match a fine mantel carved by Samuel McIntire of Salem. The kitchen had pine sheathing from a house built in 1730, and the ceiling was a reproduction of the rough unplastered work so common in farm buildings. Dow's master-touch could be seen in the parlor where he placed a Salem newspaper of 1800 on a table with a pair of silver-horned spectacles. The obvious intention here was to give the visitor the idea that someone had just removed his spectacles and left them on the table with his newspaper.[4]

The influence of the three period rooms was far greater than Dow imagined it could be. In 1910, three important officials of the Metropolitan Museum of Art in New York City visited the Essex Institute in order to see how American furniture would look in rooms with early woodwork. Shortly afterward, the Metropolitan purchased a large collection of American furniture with the intention of buying old paneling to use in period rooms. In 1924, the American Wing of the Metropolitan opened with a large number of exhibitions based on the models that Dow had provided in Salem.

Since he had been the pioneer in using old woodwork in museum displays, it was only logical that, in 1922, the Metropolitan Museum called upon Dow to help prepare the period rooms. The experience that he had acquired in working on seventeenth-century structures stood him in good stead in New York, where he reproduced several rooms typical of the first hundred years of the colonies. In his earlier restorations or reconstructions, Dow had studied the evidence in front of him with the eye of a detective. An architect who knew Dow described this process many years later: "[Dow was] minutely inspecting every nail-hole, every mortise or cut in the old framework, or prying beneath later applications of lathe and plaster in order to seek out patiently each shred of evidence."[5]

Two years after the alcoves were completed in the Essex Institute, Dow found a rare historical bargain available for his next experiment in illustrating the life of the past. Essex County had bought a house built in 1685 with the intention of tearing it down in order to clear a lot for a new jail. Dow discovered that the Ward House (as it was known) could be had for the cost of moving it to the grounds of the Essex Institute. He persuaded several members of the institute to assist financially in this effort, and then he set to work to make the Ward House the central feature of his new backyard museum. Dow had been in Europe during the summer of 1909 and had returned with new ideas on how a museum should educate the visiting public. Once he had restored the interior of the Ward House and rebuilt the chimney, Dow put these theories into practice. During the summer months, he hired some ladies to live in the second floor of the house in order to receive visitors who rang the cowbell at the door. These guides, dressed in homespun, showed their guests a dining room and a kitchen furnished with old utensils and then moved to the rear portion of the house where Dow had constructed a spinning room and a "cent-shop" (or general store). Next to the Ward House he placed an old cobbler's shop and a cupola from a shipowner's home. The sides of the yard were lined with porches and other architectural fragments from Salem houses. The public was so enthusiastic about the exhibition that a movie company came to Salem in 1914 to record the ladies in the 1685 house. Within a decade, other outdoor museums appeared in New Salem, Illinois, and Augusta, Maine.

At about this time, a whole new field was opening up for George Francis Dow. People were recognizing his experience in restoring old houses. The Topsfield Historical Society turned to him in 1913 to help carry out a restoration of the Parson Capen House, built in 1683. Dow won the praise of both architects and historians when he opened the house in January of 1914 with a "colonial" meal that was eaten from wooden plates with pewter knives and spoons. Within a few years, Dow was called upon to supervise restorations in several places in Essex County and as far away as Rhode Island and Maine. By 1922, he was able to advertise himself as a man who "has planned and superintended the restoration" of a number of New England houses.[6]

A sharp break in Dow's career came in 1918, when he left the Essex Institute after twenty years of service, and went to Boston to work for the Society for the Preservation of New England Antiquities as curator of its museum and editor of its *Bulletin,* which he renamed *Old-Time New England.* He spent three days a week in Boston, cataloging objects, arranging museum cases, and handling the bookkeeping for the society. The rest of the week he was in libraries going through old newspapers and documents or at home in Topsfield working on books and articles having to do with various aspects of history. This is essentially the way in which he spent the last eighteen years of his life—but the output of these years would stagger any normal person.

To begin with, George Francis Dow transformed *Old-Time*

George Francis Dow

New England into a periodical that dealt with every aspect of life in New England as illustrated by relics or documents. He contributed nearly twenty major articles himself and inserted columns that included a hoard of material that he had "gleaned" from newspapers. In several cases, he skillfully inserted into *Old-Time New England* sections of books that he was about to publish.

Once he was freed of his day-to-day responsibilities at the Essex Institute, Dow began to publish books that were really source collections for those who wanted to know more about different phases of American life in the past. His first book was entitled *Two Centuries of Travel in Essex County,* and it became the model for a number of his later works. He opened *Two Centuries of Travel* with a brief introduction and then reprinted several journals of trips taken in Essex County during the colonial period. After this effort, Dow formed a new organization, which he named the Marine Research Society of Salem. From 1922 to 1936, this organization published a number of books dealing with the history of New England shipping. Dow was actually in partnership in the new society with a friend in Topsfield, William A. Perkins, a printer who operated the Wayside Press.

When the three hundredth anniversary of Salem was to be celebrated in 1930, the city fathers decided to reconstruct a village depicting the Salem of 1630 in a park. On the strength of his reputation and experience, Dow was selected to do the research for the reconstruction and supervise the actual building operation. He did not stop there, but went on to write a detailed booklet on life in Salem during its first years. George Francis Dow always poured all of his tremendous energies into a task once he accepted it. Salem's Pioneer Village opened with a pageant performed by townspeople dressed in period costumes that met Dow's specifications. In the park were several wigwams built to match old descriptions, with one of them left unfinished so that visitors could see how the Indians of New England had built their homes. Dow also tried to illustrate several crafts of the first settlers, such as woodworking and the boiling of sea water for making salt.

Whenever Dow became a member of an organization, he attempted to put it on a businesslike footing and then initiated a publications program. He was so aware of the value of written records that he could not sit idly by and watch important events go unrecorded. In 1916, he joined an exclusive group of collectors known as the Walpole Society and convinced the group that they should pay for publishing an account of their meetings and trips. By 1926, his fellow Walpoleans permitted him to print a *Walpole Society Notebook* to serve as an annual report on the activities of the society, as well as an outlet for members who had articles to contribute. For eight years he supervised this activity.

During his years with the Society for the Preservation of New England Antiquities, Dow urged the society to sponsor the publication of books. Finally, at the very end of his own career, he succeeded when the society published his last great book, *Everyday Life in Massachusetts Bay Colony,* in 1935. This volume exhibited all of the scholarship and breadth of view that Dow himself had attained. The first part consisted of a study of all phases of life from the voyage over from England to the games that the Puritans played in the Massachusetts Bay Colony. There followed a host of appendices that included all types of old documents and advertisements. Dow could never resist the temptation to let the seventeenth and eighteenth centuries speak for themselves.

George Francis Dow was a most active citizen, and he was often rewarded with positions of responsibility and leadership. He centered his activities in Topsfield even though he worked in Salem and Boston, and never gave up his position of secretary of the Topsfield Historical Society, where he remained

George Francis Dow

a leader all through his life. Between 1894 and 1936, he published and edited thirty volumes of *The Historical Collections of the Topsfield Historical Society,* most of which contained articles by him. During his lifetime, he served on seven different town boards and was a trustee of the local library, town auditor, selectman, park commissioner, cemetery commissioner, trust fund commissioner, and a member of the school committee. He was the leader in a movement to build a new town library in the 1930's, and he helped to supervise that job. As park commissioner during the early years of the depression, he managed to have the town beautify the village green.

There is no question that George Francis Dow's sudden death on June 5, 1936, came as a shock to his friends and fellow-citizens. They realized more than ever that he had been a driving force in the improvement of Topsfield. Some admitted that at times he had been almost too determined in pushing projects that he wanted, but they had to confess that the results were always favorable.

Some people recognized that Dow was really a figure of national importance because of his widespread influence. Scholars in the Boston and Salem area mourned his passing because he had been the best friend they could have had—a ready source of information. One man wrote to a Boston newspaper that he remembered coming to Dow's office time after time to be greeted with the announcement, "Oh, I was just thinking of you! I've got some notes here I think you'll be interested in."[7] Naturally, these notes came from diaries or newspapers that he had just been scanning. Fortunately, George Francis Dow never became so impressed with his own accomplishments that he could not learn from others. He made it clear that he would welcome any bits of knowledge that people might want to share with him. Dow was so sure of the importance of studying history that he probably never asked himself exactly why he did it—he merely referred to himself as a "builder." There probably could not be a better title for a dedicated antiquary.

SOURCES AND NOTES

The major sources are (1) some letters in the S.P.N.E.A. files in Boston, (2) the Annual Reports for the Essex Institute from 1898 to 1918, (3) the *Walpole Society Notebook* for 1947, (4) *Bulletin* of the Metropolitan Museum for Nov., 1922, and Nov., 1924, (5) an obituary in Vol. XXX of the *Historical Collections of the Topsfield Historical Society*, (6) three letters from people who knew Dow in Salem and Topsfield, and (7) a Souvenir Program of the Topsfield Tercentenary.

1. George Francis Dow, "Report of the Secretary," *Annual Report of the Essex Institute* (1906), p. 16.
2. *Ibid.* (1900), p. 20.
3. *Ibid.* (1907), p. 17.
4. George Francis Dow, "Museums and the Preservation of Houses," *Bulletin of the Metropolitan Museum of Art*, XVII (Nov., 1922) Part II, pp. 16, 17.
5. J. Frederick Kelly, "Time Stone Farm," *Walpole Society Notebook, 1946*, p. 41.
6. Advertisement on back page, *Old-Time New England*, XIII (July, 1922).
7. Letter from John P. Brown, in an unknown newspaper, June 29, 1936, clipping in the files of the Society for the Preservation of New England Antiquities, Boston.

IV. The Special Collection

Henry Edwards Huntington

by John E. Pomfret

The Henry E. Huntington Library and Art Gallery is located in San Marino, California, near the southern border of Pasadena in Los Angeles County. It is housed on an estate of 208 acres, formerly part of a 550-acre citrus ranch. Seventy-five acres have been landscaped and developed into a series of noteworthy botanical gardens, including the Desert Plant Garden, the Palm Garden, the North Vista (azaleas and camellias), the Shakespeare Garden, the Rose Garden, the Japanese Garden, and the Camellia Garden. The principal buildings are the Art Gallery (formerly the home of Huntington) and the Library.

The Huntington Library, as this complex is popularly known, consists, in addition to the botanical gardens, of the following components: a research library in the humanities that is visited by scores of American and British scholars—a library that includes also some of the rarest books and manuscripts in the world, the joy of hundreds of collectors; a research department whose members are engaged in the writing of books based on the Huntington Library collections; a publications department; and an art gallery that specializes in eighteenth-century English paintings and drawings, sixteenth- to eighteenth-century English silver, and eighteenth-century French furniture, sculpture, and ceramics. All this is in large measure the creation of a modest and unassuming man, Henry E. Huntington.

Henry Edwards Huntington was born in Oneonta, New York, on February 27, 1850. He was the fourth of seven children of Solon and Harriet (Saunders) Huntington. His father had "migrated west" from Connecticut and chosen Oneonta, in central New York on the upper Susquehanna, as a promising business town. He had opened a general store and, after two years, had admitted to partnership his younger brother, Collis P. Huntington, the future railroad tycoon. As Oneonta, a town of two thousand inhabitants, grew, the business prospered. Solon Huntington was soon a respected citizen and showed his faith in the community by investing his money in land.

Little is known of the early life of Henry Huntington. He attended a private academy in Oneonta and was a conscientious and successful student. He grew rapidly and attained his full stature of over six feet at an early age. He became known as "Ed" to his friends, and this appellation lasted a lifetime. His dominant interests were practical, and even as a boy, he earned his pocket money by working in the store. Business fascinated him, and he made no effort to secure a college education. He determined to learn the hardware business, and to that end, he went to New York to obtain a job with a leading hardware company. At the age of twenty, he went to work as a porter, the only job that was open to him.

As he wrote his mother after a few months, he had a hard time making a living. He called upon Collis P. Huntington, who was then in New York arranging the financing the Central Pacific Railroad. His uncle offered him aid, but the younger Huntington refused, saying that a man of twenty-one should be self-supporting. Collis Huntington formed a good opinion of his nephew, and in 1871, his uncle offered him a job managing a sawmill in St. Albans, West Virginia. The mill was engaged in the cutting of railroad ties, and from this time on, Huntington's career was connected with railroads and transportation. There also began an association with his uncle that lasted, with few interruptions, until his uncle's death in 1900.

In his first foray into the business world, Huntington moved swiftly and characteristically. At the sawmill, he effected improvements and economies, with the result that the enterprise survived the Panic of 1873. Huntington first purchased a small share in the business, then became the sole owner. In November, 1873, he married Mary Alice Prentice of Sacramento at her uncle's home in Newark, New Jersey. Eventually four children were born: a son, Howard Edwards, and three daughters, Clara, Elizabeth, and Marian. (This marriage terminated in divorce in 1906.) In 1876, the young millowner sold out and returned to Oneonta to assist his father in a rapidly growing business. He was not to remain there for long for, in 1881, his uncle Collis appointed him superintendent of construction of the Chesapeake, Ohio & South Western Railroad, with instructions to complete the section of railroad from Trimble, Tennessee, to Covington, Kentucky. Again, Huntington demonstrated his executive ability. Legend has it that, though the men worked hard, Huntington never stopped working.

In 1886, his uncle offered him a more difficult assignment, the management of the Kentucky Central. Here he made a name for himself as a railroad official, and by 1890, railroad men felt it necessary to distinguish between the Huntingtons, "C. P." and "H. E." Through the reorganization of the Kentucky Central, Huntington for the first time amassed considerable capital. In 1892, H. E., at his uncle's bidding, moved to San Francisco to represent the Huntington interests on the Pacific Coast and to share in the management of the Southern Pacific Railroad, the successor of the Central Pacific. His was not an easy task, for the other members of the Big Four, Leland Stanford, Mark Hopkins, and Charles Crocker, viewed his presence with some misgiving. Nevertheless, H. E. discharged his responsibilities magnificently until his uncle's sudden death in August, 1900. The key to his success in railroading has been epitomized as insistence upon high standards of maintenance and his ability to build a loyal and efficient personnel. He himself developed qualities of courage, independence, and loyalty to a high degree, and he proved that his business abilities were not dependent upon the favors of his uncle.

In 1892, on his way to San Francisco, Huntington stopped off at Los Angeles and was entertained at the ranch of J. De Barth Shorb, "San Marino." He was enchanted with the ranch and the surrounding countryside. During his years in California, he had journeyed throughout the state in order to observe with his own eyes its potentialities for the future and became convinced that southern California had the most promising prospects. One of his tasks in the north during the lifetime of Collis P. Huntington was the management of several electric railways in San Francisco. He perceived excellent possibilities in constructing lines of electric railways in areas of great potential growth. With this in mind, after his uncle's death, he transferred his headquarters from San Francisco to Los Angeles.

Aware of the inadequacy of the local service in Los Angeles and its vicinity, Mr. Huntington used his knowledge and experience to fashion a great metropolitan railroad system to serve greater Los Angeles. Within ten years, he had created an urban and interurban system surpassing any heretofore known or imagined. He organized the Los Angeles railway system providing service within the city (City Railway, Los Angeles Railway), and his interurban network (Pacific Electric Railway) served the whole "Orange Empire" from San Bernardino to Long Beach and other coastal cities. His "red cars" became a transportation symbol in southern California, and the last run (to Long Beach) was not withdrawn until 1963.

Mr. Huntington was involved in a number of other giant business enterprises. His landholdings were prodigious, leading to the founding of entire new towns. He was interested in the development of water power and electric utilities. At one time, he served on as many as sixty corporation boards. During the period 1900 to 1910, he was considered one of the outstanding figures of southern California. During this decade of his greatest activity, the population of Los Angeles had tripled. In 1908, Huntington announced his decision to retire from active business. In 1910, he sold the Pacific Electric system to the Southern Pacific Company. In reality, he was never entirely free from business, for the stewardship, alone, of his vast holdings entailed large responsibilities.

Huntington could now turn toward his underlying interest: that of acquiring rare books, manuscripts, and works of art. He was a born collector with an instinctive appreciation of fine things. His book collecting was begun at St. Albans, West Virginia, where he began by buying first editions of his favorite authors. After some years of experience, he adopted higher standards and disposed of his poorer copies. Only one book from the early period, one of his boyhood books, did he keep to the end. The earliest acquisitions incorporated in the present Huntington Library were those made after 1900. Huntington was attracted first to the arts of bookmaking—to printing, illustrating, and binding. For example, he secured a complete set of works printed at the Kelmscott Press and extensive collections of the works of Alken, Rowlandson, and the Cruikshanks. During this period, he evinced a fondness for beautifully printed and handsomely bound books, illuminated manuscripts, and incunabula. He began to show leanings toward English literature and Americana.

After his so-called retirement, Huntington spent lavishly in augmenting his collections. His method was unique: to purchase when possible whole libraries and later eliminate duplicates and other unwanted items. The size and cost of a collection were secondary items, while the decisive considerations were scope, quality, and condition. Innumerable gaps were filled by individual or small group purchases when opportunity afforded. For example, there were eighty sources for the five hundred titles entered under the name of William Shakespeare. Forty per cent came from a dozen en bloc purchases, 40 per cent from thirty auction sales, and the remainder from dealers. Mr. Huntington employed no corps of agents to search out and to purchase books and manuscripts; he simply took advantage of the many fine opportunities on the open market. In this way, the great Church, Hoe, Huth, and Britwell library collections, each of which had required a lifetime to assemble, came into his possession. For example, the Church Collection, which consisted of 2,133 rare books and manuscripts in English and American history, was bought en bloc for $1,000,000.

In all his purchases, Huntington relied upon expert advice. In his book and manuscript purchases, he sought advice from George D. Smith and, after Smith's death in 1920, from Dr. A. S. Rosenbach. When he began to collect paintings, he turned to Sir Joseph Duveen, later (1933) Lord Duveen. George Smith, who had been in the book business from boyhood, had, by 1910, attained a commanding position in the rare-book trade. He knew little about the contents of the books he handled, but his long experience had given him a remarkable knowledge of the rarity and value of books and manuscripts. His audacity in buying, his unaffectedness, and his loyalty to his patrons appealed greatly to Huntington, who trusted Smith's judgment highly. He employed him more than any other agent and entrusted him with the negotiations preceding the majority of his purchases. Huntington was often chided by fellow collectors regarding the wisdom of paying the prices he did. But before his death, his scale of book prices was generally exceeded. "I know," he said more than once, "that I have often paid too much for books, but, on the other hand, I have just as often been lucky in getting bargains."

Henry Edwards Huntington

In 1902, Huntington purchased "San Marino," the ranch of 550 acres, where ten years before he had been entertained by his friend J. De Barth Shorb. (It was later reduced to its present 208 acres.) It lay partly in Pasadena, partly in what is now San Marino, and was situated about eleven miles from Los Angeles. The improvements needed at the ranch provided him with relaxing diversions. Assisted by his German-trained superintendent, William Hertrich, Huntington utilized sections of the ranch to determine what horticultural specimens from other parts of the world could be grown in southern California. On this estate, for example, the first avocados in California were grown commercially. The development of a collection of palms and cycads and a large collection of cacti and other succulents, more than 25,000 in number, became ultimately one of the world's greatest desert plant gardens. In 1906, Huntington began planning a spacious house at "San Marino." It was completed in 1910.

Despite his interest in English books and paintings, Huntington was not greatly attracted by foreign travel. Many of his friendships revolved about his book-collecting hobby. He participated in organizing the Hobby Club in New York, and in 1911, he joined the Grolier Club. After his home was erected, "San Marino" became for him a self-sufficient world. In 1913, on the occasion of his second marriage in Paris to his aunt, Arabella Huntington, the former Mrs. Collis P. Huntington, he visited Europe for the first time. For a few seasons, he occupied a château near Paris, a city Mrs. Huntington cherished, and just before World War I, he visited England.

By 1915, Huntington's library had grown to such proportions —over forty thousand books—that it became necessary to employ a professional librarian. His collection had far outgrown his New York quarters at the Metropolitan Club and—after his second marriage—his home on 57th Street, and hundreds were in storage. The post of librarian went to Dr. George Watson Cole, the cataloguer of the Church Collection. Dr. Cole assembled a small staff of competent men, and the work of cataloguing began. Acquisitions were made at such a rate that the group grew to twelve, all that the available space in his New York house could accommodate. In his visits to New York, Huntington could be found more frequently in his library with George Smith and other bookdealers than anywhere else. Here also he would entertain his fellow bibliophiles and show them his choicest treasures. A retiring person by nature, he delighted in talking with a sympathetic listener about his collections.

Unlike other collectors, Huntington never attempted to retain more than one copy of a rare book, although he instructed his staff to undertake a careful study of all duplicates and to keep any variant editions. When the bulk of this work of collation was completed in 1916, the first auction of his duplicates was held. In all, fifteen sales were conducted, and as a result, Mr. Huntington garnered a total of a half million dollars, which was used for the purchase of new items. In an article published in 1917, the New York *Times* stated that Huntington had spent six million dollars on his library in the six preceding years, and this was no exaggeration. In the recently published biography of Dr. Rosenbach, it is revealed that Huntington paid $4,333,000 to him alone for books and manuscripts.

With the completion of his "San Marino" home, Huntington was confronted with an important decision: whether to move his books to California, which would entail the construction of a library building; or whether, at this point, to turn his collections over to an institution. After several years of deliberation, he determined to erect a library at "San Marino" and to make a gift of his collections to the people of California in the form of a trust. In 1919, the deeds of trust creating the Henry E. Huntington Library and Art Gallery were drawn up, and about the same time, construction was begun on the library building. The first board of trustees consisted of his son, Howard; Archer M. Huntington, a stepson and founder of the Hispanic Society of

Henry Edwards Huntington

America; Dr. George Ellery Hale, director of Mt. Wilson Observatory; George S. Patton, father of General Patton of World War II fame; and William E. Dunn, Huntington's lawyer. Others who have served through the years on the board include Henry M. Robinson, financier; the Honorable Herbert Hoover; Dr. Robert A. Millikan, the physicist; Dr. Henry S. Pritchett, president of the Carnegie Foundation; and Dr. J. E. Wallace Sterling, president of Stanford University.

The transfer of Huntington's collections from New York to "San Marino" caused much comment in the press. The opinion was generally expressed that his treasures would be more appreciated and utilized by scholars on the East Coast than in the Far West. But Huntington was, as usual, looking far ahead, and he foresaw great intellectual development in his adopted region. His faith has been borne out. After the opening of the Huntington Library, higher education took giant strides in the Far West and the Southwest. In southern California, the establishment of graduate departments in many institutions heightened the responsibility of the Huntington Library in its services to scholars. At the present time, humanists on the faculties of thirty-five neighboring institutions depend on the Huntington Library for their research activities. Moreover, the choicest treasures of the library have been on public exhibition for several score years and have been seen by millions of people.

Huntington witnessed the opening of the library building—now much enlarged—and met the first scholars who came to examine his rare books and manuscripts. While planning the library building, he had said, "I perhaps shall not live to welcome them, but... when they come... it is my desire to make their goal worthwhile." During the last seven years of his life, he continued his purchases, but under the influence of George Hale, a trustee, and other members of the scholarly community, his views changed radically. His emphasis in purchasing turned more and more toward concentration in the broad fields of English and American history and literature. Under his librarians, efforts were made to fill in gaps in the collections, and in answer to the needs of scholars, a beginning was made in building up what is now a comprehensive reference library.

In 1925, the trustees recommended to Huntington the adoption of a program for the encouragement of research. Dr. Max Farrand, formerly a distinguished professor of American history at Yale University, was invited to the library as the first research associate. He was requested to draft a plan that would enable the library to become a research institution devoted to the study of Anglo-American civilization. Dr. Farrand's recommendations were adopted by the board, and he was appointed director of research. With Farrand came the appointment of research associates, each a specialist in one of the major fields of the library's collections; a great expansion of the library's staff, including the appointment of several bibliographers; a systematic building of the reference collections; the inauguration of a fellowship and grant-in-aid program; the institution of research seminars for visiting scholars; and a program of publishing the manuscript treasures of the library and the research findings of scholars studying at the library. Since then, books, bibliographical lists, and bulletins reproducing rare manuscript materials have appeared regularly. *The Huntington Library Quarterly* began publication in 1937. At the present time, about one thousand scholars work at the library each year, for periods varying from a week to a year.

Huntington never interfered with the decisions of his board of trustees. The board consulted him frequently about policy, and he took a lively interest in everything that went on in the institution. He lived in his "San Marino" home until his death on May 23, 1927. Despite vast expenditures for his collections and his benefactions, his estate was valued at $40,000,000. His wife Arabella had died in 1924. In her memory, Huntington established, in a wing of the library, a fine collection of Renais-

Henry Edwards Huntington

sance paintings, French furniture, Sèvres ware, and French sculptures—her favorite *objets d'art*.

In 1923, the trustees persuaded Huntington that he must set up an endowment fund to enable the institution to operate through future years. From 1923 to 1928, he transferred equities and other assets with a book value of $8,000,000 to the institution. Thanks to able management by succeeding boards of trustees, the institution has never experienced serious financial difficulties, despite large outlays for major improvements and personnel expansion.

The creation of the Henry E. Huntington Library and Art Gallery, together with its renowned botanical gardens, represented the realization of long-cherished ideals and brought Huntington great satisfaction during the closing years of his life. A village boy, he had worked hard all his life, and through his early and mature years, he devoted from eighteen to twenty hours a day to the tasks before him. He was a key man in the development of the megalopolis now known as southern California. Although he concentrated his philanthropy on the institution bearing his name, Huntington lent his aid to many public-spirited causes. In southern California, he was highly respected as a man of great integrity, and, unlike many business barons of his day, his name was never associated with unscrupulous business practices. Huntington was an imposing man but, in many ways, a shy man. He made few public addresses and was never a candidate for public office. He was a modest man. When friends requested him to have an official biography written he replied: "No, never. I have been approached regarding a biography, but I do not want that. This Library will tell the story. It represents the reward of all the work I have ever done and the realization of much happiness."

Bella C. Landauer

by James J. Heslin

New Yorkers, presumably, are immune to unusual sights in their city, but some, as they waited at the bus stop in front of The New-York Historical Society, were visibly startled when they saw a well-dressed, elderly lady alight from a taxi at 9:00 A.M. clutching several empty whiskey bottles. It is doubtful that Mrs. Bella C. Landauer was aware of the impression she created as she moved with dignity up the steps and into the society's building. Had she noticed the reaction of the bystanders, she probably would have calmly explained that the whiskey bottles were being added to her collections, and she would have concluded by asking members of her audience to bring to her any old advertising material they might happen to have.

Mrs. Landauer's unending interest in all odds and ends of advertising matter not only earned for her the sobriquet of "Parsley and Parsnips," but also renown for having amassed one of the country's significant collections of material relating to American advertising. Even though most merchants, until 1870, thought advertising to be undignified, it was an important factor in the development of American business and industry. Advertisements mirror the customs, manners, values, and tastes of an era, making yesterday's advertising part of social history, and

Bella C. Landauer

Mrs. Landauer believed that in no other period in this country did advertising picture so accurately the social history of its day as did that in the nineteenth-century. When eyebrows were raised at some of the items she collected, Mrs. Landauer declared: "All collectors gather good items, but . . . whose judgment is infallible? What may be rejected as inconsequential trash, I gather and preserve as a nucleus for historic reconstruction." Thus, it was a source of considerable gratification to Mrs. Landauer when she first became aware that her collection, much of it composed of items spurned by others, was of importance to historians.

Initially, Mrs. Landauer began collecting without any intention of forming what eventually became one of the major collections of business and professional advertising materials in the United States. After an illness precipitated by her extensive volunteer work during World War I, Mrs. Landauer was advised by her physician to interest herself in a hobby. As so often happens, Mrs. Landauer postponed acting on this advice, and it was some time later, quite by chance, that she finally found her "hobby."

On a hot summer day in 1923, Mrs. Landauer's telephone rang and a picture-framer with whom she had had business dealings on various occasions told a woeful tale of a young man who was in desperate financial straits and wanted to sell a portfolio of prints and bookplates. Knowing little about bookplates but moved by the plight of the young man, Mrs. Landauer purchased the portfolio for one hundred dollars.

That same evening, "for lack of a better occupation on a hot night," Mrs. Landauer studied her purchase, and thus, at the age of forty-eight, she embarked on what was to be her major interest for the remainder of her long life. She soon began to visit bookstores in New York, carrying folders of her bookplates with her. In one bookstore, to the proprietor's astonishment, Mrs. Landauer rejected one after another of the bookplates of-

Keepers of the Past

fered to her, explaining to the bewildered man that she owned duplicates of what he had to sell. When he asked Mrs. Landauer where she had purchased her bookplates and she described the circumstances, the dealer interrupted her excitedly to say that the young man who sold her the bookplates was light-fingered; the bookplates had been stolen from the very shop in which Mrs. Landauer was now seated. There is no evidence that the proprietor ever attempted to recover his property and, as Mrs. Landauer wryly expressed it, "...my start in life as a collector came through acquiring stolen goods."

As her knowledge of the field increased, Mrs. Landauer soon heard of other collectors, and she wrote to one of them, William E. Baille, an authority on bookplates, concerning her new-found interest. Baille graciously invited Mrs. Landauer to join him and his wife for lunch, and so began a long and pleasant relationship in which Baille undertook to instruct his eager pupil in the fine points of bookplates.

Gradually, Mrs. Landauer began to extend her collecting to nineteenth-century trade cards. These cards carried advertisements of various businesses and professions and were commonly used to make known the attributes of manufacturers, railroads, stores, restaurants, bookshops, law firms—almost every conceivable kind of industry and service. They ranged in size from one to five inches high by two to seven inches wide and were often gaily colored, and frequently illustrated and elaborately printed. In their day, these cards served as effective advertising since they were distributed by retailers and wholesalers and had a wide circulation in towns as well as in the larger centers. All manner of subjects—humor, patriotism, sports, domesticity—were utilized in advertising goods and services on trade cards.

At first, Baille viewed this new interest of his friend with misgiving. In 1924, he wrote to Mrs. Landauer: "My congratulations on your purchase...but alas, I am sore afraid you are hankering after strange gods and dissipating a real affection for

Bella C. Landauer

bookplates." But Mrs. Landauer had embarked on what was to be her real pursuit—the collection of advertising material. When Baille recognized that this was an area that could be of importance in the future, he reconciled himself to Mrs. Landauer's new interests and began to offer suggestions. "Dear Lady of the many distracting occupations," he wrote, "in your increasing quest...has it ever occurred to you that hotels are in trade and that the picture cards they issue, might be safely included in such a collection as you are making. One hundred years from now they should be interesting."

Not everyone was as understanding as Baille. There were those who scorned Mrs. Landauer's broadened collecting policy. One lady loftily denounced this hobby as absurd, and a gentleman once remarked: "I hear you are only collecting from scrapbaskets."

Mrs. Landauer perservered despite these unsympathetic views, and as her collection slowly grew in size, bookdealers and auctioneers began to watch for items of interest to her. So diligent was she in her collecting that in a short time Mrs. Landauer had reached the point where she was able to dispose of duplicate trade cards. Seated at her desk, flanked by two empty hat boxes, she consigned duplicates to these receptacles, and, when filled, one box was dispatched to the Harvard Business Library and the other to the Print Department of the Metropolitan Museum of Art in New York.

In time, Mrs. Landauer became interested in a variety of new items, such as American sheet music, aeronautical history, and theater programs. When asked how she developed these new interests, Mrs. Landauer cheerfully replied, "Some fireworks shoot off rockets in all directions." But, however diverse her collecting, it was never erratic; it was the advertising related to these new fields that really interested her.

Mrs. Landauer's collection of sheet music was acquired for the advertising and illustrations on the covers. A sizeable pro-

Keepers of the Past

portion of this material related to New York City because, as Mrs. Landauer viewed it, New York is the advertising capital of the United States. Sentiment, however, may have exerted some influence. Mrs. Landauer was born in New York, she was educated in private schools in the city, and, despite wide travel abroad—and a great love for Paris—New York was her city and always first in her affection.

In 1951, she published a volume entitled *My City 'tis of Thee: New York on Sheet Music Covers,* and her selection of eighty pieces of sheet music from her large collection reflected the warmth with which she regarded New York. Included were the *Fifth Avenue Polka,* published in 1852; the *Union Park Schottisch* (c. 1850); the *Staten Island Polka-Mazurka;* and *New-York Crystal Palace Polka* (1852); and a piece called *A Waltz on the Beautiful Hudson.*

An evidence of how some fireworks shoot off rockets in all directions was Mrs. Landauer's material relating to her favorite playwright, Eugene O'Neill. This collection, consisting of five scrapbooks of theater programs from American and European theaters, sixty-eight letters (over half written by O'Neill), rare photographs, and twenty-four first editions of his plays, was donated by Mrs. Landauer, in 1951, to the library of Dartmouth College, the school from which her son James had graduated in 1923.

To Mrs. Landauer's delight, it seemed that whenever she acquired one item, others followed. Just as her collection of Eugene O'Neill material grew to significant proportions, so too did another collection that reflected her interest—aviation. In due course, Mrs. Landauer presented this material to the Institute of Aeronautical Sciences in New York, which elected her a benefactor in 1941.

Every collector has moments of prescience when he senses that an item may be eluding his grasp, and Mrs. Landauer, more than once, almost missed an item upon which she had set her

Bella C. Landauer

heart. One of these experiences concerned the trade card of Francis Hopkinson of Philadelphia—one of the Signers of the Declaration of Independence. This card, advertising cloth for sale by Hopkinson, was signed by him on the reverse side and included the date, September 24, 1769. When Mrs. Landauer saw this card, she was determined to purchase it. Uncertain as to whether or not she could be present at the sale that was to be held at a prominent auction gallery in New York, Mrs. Landauer left a top bid of twenty-five dollars. As evening approached, she became uneasy and suddenly decided to visit the gallery to watch the proceedings. Eventually, the trade card came up for sale and her twenty-five dollar bid was soon surpassed. The chase was on, and stimulated by the collector's instinct, Mrs. Landauer plunged in and bid up and up until the card was hers for the sum of one hundred and fifty dollars! Little did she realize at the time that the opposing bidder was the noted book dealer, Dr. A. S. W. Rosenbach. When the news of this transaction spread among the dealers and auctioneers, Mrs. Landauer became aware that she had "arrived" as a collector.

In 1927, Mrs. Landauer offered her collection of book plates and trade cards to the library of The New-York Historical Society in return for the privilege of serving as curator of the collection—an offer that was quickly accepted. Mr. Alexander J. Wall, the society's director at that time, wrote later, in the *Annual Report for 1935,* "...the collection promised to be of lasting benefit not only to members...of the craft of printing, but in some considerable measure to historians, sociologists, psychologists, and indeed all who have to conduct research into events, fashions, or any of the social and intellectual movements which have found expression in or received impetus from printed documents other than books.... Such records could not have come into existence unless they had...expressed fundamental human traits."

Keepers of the Past

When Mrs. Landauer transferred her collection from her apartment to the society, there were over 100,000 items relating to advertising by industries and business firms. Over the years, the collection has expanded until there are now approximately 400,000 pieces, among which are: broadsides, posters, trade cards, buttons, and badges. Included also are: paperweights, menus, valentines, invitations, lottery tickets, railroad timetables, department store catalogues, music sheets, wine labels, announcements of social events, and theater programs. Most of the items, except for large broadsides and posters are pasted in large, eighty-page folio volumes. Each page in these folio volumes measures fifteen by twenty inches and contains from one to twenty items, depending upon size. All of the items relating to a particular subject appear together and, with the aid of a subject list compiled by Mrs. Landauer, it is relatively easy to find what is wanted.

When Mrs. Landauer presented her collection to The New-York Historical Society in 1927, the only space available for it was an unused kitchen on the third floor of the building. For a number of years, however, Mrs. Landauer persevered in these limited quarters, enlarging her collections, arranging her "treasures" as best she could, until 1939, when additions to the building made it possible to increase the area allotted to her. This permitted more people to see and use the material, which pleased Mrs. Landauer greatly, not because it confirmed her judgment as a collector, since she was essentially too modest to gloat over this fact, but because it was now possible for many historians to comprehend the scope of advertising in the United States during the last century. As the collection became better known, it inevitably attracted more material from generous donors, and Mrs. Landauer herself continued energetically to collect whenever possible for the remainder of her life.

The expansion of the society's building and the increased use of the materials by researchers made inroads on Mrs. Landauer's

Bella C. Landauer

time as curator of her collection—inroads that she accepted cheerfully. She was kept busy answering telephone calls and writing letters in response to questions from persons seeking information, cataloging her collections, helping scholars who visited the building in search of data about early advertising, and dealing with those who came to her with material to donate or to sell. Her devotion to the collection is demonstrated by the fact that she spent part of each day, including Sunday, at the society.

Some of the items in this collection may intrigue later generations since they portray social customs that have altered considerably during the past fifty to seventy-five years. At one time, for example, a strict and rigid code governed every detail of the funeral customs, and an interest in these details, far from being morbid, is educational.

Mrs. Landauer was attracted one day by an arresting notice advertising "Burial Lots only $15.00.—payable at $2. a month." These lots were described as having unrivalled views and good soil although neither of these selling points could have been of much concern to the deceased. This advertisement, issued about 1849 by the New York Bay Cemetery Company, stimulated Mrs. Landauer to search for more material on the subject. In her research, she discovered that as early as 1684, in New York, there was a public "Inviter to Funerals," appointed by the governor, and such "Inviters" were "obliged to attend the burial of the poor." When funerals became private affairs about fifty years later, an elaborate code of etiquette developed which included the use of written invitations and mourning cards, delivered by messenger. Only those specifically invited could attend. By the turn of the nineteenth century, funeral announcements were printed in the newspapers, eliminating the need for hired messengers, but as late as the middle of the nineteenth century, it was still socially proper to write to near friends and relatives of the deceased announcing a death. Just as the greeting card of the twentieth century has replaced much of the written correspon-

Keepers of the Past

dence of an earlier period relating to birthdays and similar events, so did commercially-printed funeral cards replace hand-written death announcements during the last half of the nineteenth century. These funeral cards were often quite elaborate, and although writers of etiquette books tended to deplore the custom, Americans, always in a hurry, were quick to use them.

In the more leisurely nineteenth century there was time for ceremony, formality, and ritual—aspects reflected in some of the customs of the age. Mrs. Landauer commented, when discussing the large collection of funeral items that she had acquired, that they indicated a different philosophy toward death. She believed that ceremonies associated with death in former times were no indication that feelings of grief were any deeper than those of our own, but she deplored the haste attending many of the present customs. Mrs. Landauer was fond of quoting a remark she once heard, apropos of the hustle and bustle of the modern age and its relation to funerals: "Nowadays, in case of death, no one stays at home but the corpse."

The curiosities relating to funerals are but a portion of Mrs. Landauer's odd and historically interesting treasures. Searching through her collections, a picture of an earlier day emerges from which we can make a number of judgments. We find that, in the nineteenth century, advertisers did not appeal merely to the lowest common denominator but aimed also at a highly literate audience: for example, purveyors of cigars used the names of books and authors on the wrappers of their wares; some advertisements included pictures of American writers; and the virtues of tobacco and soap were often extolled in parodies of well-known poems by literary figures such as Longfellow. Mrs. Landauer once explained, in emphasizing the fact that literature and advertising were closely related in the nineteenth century, that it was not her intention to recommend the employment of Doctors of Literature by advertising agencies but, rather, to bring this relationship to the attention of historians.

Bella C. Landauer

To the day of her death, on April 23, 1960, at age of eighty-five, this gallant, sprightly, and wonderfully vital lady continued to collect, preserve, and make available the advertising of another day. Despite her years, her temperament never permitted tiresome reminiscences; she lived very much in the present and planned for the future. Her recollections were always meaningful and apt. When a would-be collector came to Mrs. Landauer for advice asking, "What should I collect?" she replied by telling the questioner to use his imagination, and in so doing, he might discover something new to collect—something no one else had thought of. Mrs. Landauer often added that the person who discovers a new field of collecting not only earns distinction but saves money since the early bird often collects on a shoe string. Mrs. Landauer, with a twinkle in her eye, once said:

> Last autumn's chestnuts, rather passés,
> Are now presented as marrons glacés.

SOURCES

Landauer, Bella C. "Collecting and Recollecting," *New-York Historical Society Quarterly* (July, 1959), pp. 335-49.

———. "Literary Allusions in American Advertising as Sources of Social History," *New-York Historical Society Quarterly* (July, 1947), pp. 148-49.

———. *My City 'Tis of Thee: New York City on Sheet-Music Covers.* New York, 1951.

———. "Some American Funeral Ephemera," *New-York Historical Society Quarterly* (April, 1952), pp. 221-30.

Presbrey, Frank. *The History and Development of Advertising.* Garden City, 1929.

Rowsome, Frank, Jr. *They Laughed when I Sat Down.* New York, 1959.

Wood, James Playsted. *The Story of Advertising.* New York, 1958.

V. The Historic Site

Ann Pamela Cunningham

by Charles B. Hosmer, Jr.

In studying the outstanding women of the nineteenth century, we rarely hear of the dynamic little lady who founded the first successful large patriotic organization in the United States. Ann Pamela Cunningham was not fighting for women's rights; she had a much larger object in view: the prevention of the Civil War. Our neglect of Miss Cunningham is even more ironic when we realize that without her efforts we might not have George Washington's home at Mount Vernon today.

Nothing in her background would cause one to suspect that Ann Pamela Cunningham would be destined to become a leader in later life. She was born on August 15, 1816, at Rosemont, the South Carolina plantation of her wealthy father, Captain Robert Cunningham. Apparently Ann Pamela had all of the things a girl could have wanted during the years she was growing up, and it would have been natural for her to become a typical member of the southern aristocracy. When she was seventeen, her whole world changed abruptly when she fell from a horse and suffered a severe spinal injury. Victorian etiquette prevented people from discussing "delicate" subjects, so we can only guess why Miss Cunningham was a semi-invalid most of her life. In her letters, she spoke of spending most of the winter with her head encased in pillows and scarves in order to overcome chills. Often she was too ill to write or move around, and sometimes she had to remain for long periods in a dark room. Her family wealth permitted her to visit Dr. Hugh L. Hodge in Philadelphia, one of the most noted physicians of the time, but it appeared that Ann Pamela was doomed to a lifetime of uselessness.

The second event that altered the course of her life occurred in the fall of 1853, when Miss Cunningham was thirty-seven. Her mother decided to go south for the winter while Ann Pamela remained in Philadelphia under the care of Dr. Hodge. The first letter from Mrs. Cunningham excited Ann Pamela, for it described the scene of ruin and desolation at Mount Vernon that her mother had witnessed from a passing riverboat. Mrs. Cunningham wondered if "the women of his country" could save Washington's home. Ann Pamela responded almost immediately by writing to the Charleston, South Carolina, *Mercury*, asking for help from the "Ladies of the South." When reading an appeal written in the nineteenth century, one has to realize that it was customary to be wordy even in a simple message. Perhaps this excerpt from the letter will illustrate: "...One of your countrywomen feels emboldened to appeal in the name of the Mother of Washington, and of Southern feeling and honor to all that is sympathetic and generous in your nature, to exert itself, and by your combined effort *now*, in village and country, town and city, the means may be raised from the mites of thousands of gentle hearts, upon whom his name has yet a magic spell, which will suffice to secure and retain his home and grave as a sacred spot for all coming time."[1]

In the 1850's, women were not supposed to engage in any public activities so Miss Cunningham's modesty caused her to sign the letter "A Southern Matron." She had every intention of staying behind the scenes while the American people rose en masse to her call, believing that leading a great national movement was no place for an invalid lady.

Ann Pamela Cunningham

Soon Ann Pamela Cunningham's fears for the future of Mount Vernon overcame her thoughts of weakness, retirement, and womanly pride. She had been transformed into a crusader. Fortunately, she had no idea of the difficulties that lay ahead of her, and she had many powerful allies among her friends and relations in the South. Early in 1854, equipped with sound legal advice, Miss Cunningham began to create the Mount Vernon Ladies' Association of the Union. She appointed "vice-regents" in six states and sent them subscription papers to record the names of the thousands of patriots who stood ready to save the home of the Father of His Country.

But now Ann Pamela encountered her first great obstacle in the person of John A. Washington, who owned the land she wanted. There was certainly no point in generating enthusiasm and collecting money for the Mount Vernon Association if the Washington family was unwilling to sell the estate to the ladies. Washington told Miss Cunningham that he regretted his inability to help her, but he was in the process of negotiating with the State of Virginia for the purchase of Mount Vernon. But the State of Virginia could not meet John Washington's high price for Mount Vernon ($200,000), and so the situation dragged on for years.

By the summer of 1854, the "Southern Matron" had identified herself in public, because the American people wanted to know who this lady might be. At that time, she began to form committees in the North as well as in the South, and immediately her talents as an organizer and peacemaker came into play. Unfortunately, the active committee of the Mount Vernon Association in Richmond, Virginia, began to talk too much about Virginia's part in the undertaking. Northern members objected to the implications of sectionalism, and only Ann Pamela herself was able to convince all the ladies that they were a part of a national association.

More than ever Ann Pamela Cunningham saw that she

needed allies in her work—and she won two notable converts to her cause through her persuasive powers: Edward Everett and John Washington! Edward Everett will always occupy an uncomfortable place in history as the long-winded orator who preceded Lincoln on the day of the Gettysburg Address; but that incident should not obscure the fact that Everett was the most popular public speaker of his time. Early in 1856, Miss Cunningham managed to persuade him to give an address on the character of George Washington for a Mount Vernon meeting in Richmond. Very few descriptions of the leader of the Mount Vernon Association can equal this comment from Everett's diary for March 10, 1856: "I called very early on Miss Cunningham, the Southern Matron, who has been principally active in getting up the Ladies' Mount Vernon Association. She is a confirmed invalid and confined to her chamber; but by great mental energy has contrived with infinite embarrassment and disgusts to collect subscriptions to a large amount. . . . An invalid maiden lady seems the last person to manage a difficult business, but I believe this poor little woman, dropping into the grave with a spinal complaint, has done all that has been done for the purchase of Mount Vernon."[2]

Everett was so swept up in the idealism of the Mount Vernon movement that he offered to give his address free of charge anywhere that the ladies might like to send him. In three years, he gave the speech 139 times, and the admission fees donated to the Mount Vernon fund amounted to about $50,000.

Although he was not a critic of Miss Cunningham and her followers, John A. Washington continued to be the principal obstacle to the association. Only one person could win his good will, and Ann Pamela set out bravely to do the job herself. One hot June day in 1856, she went down the Potomac by steamer to visit the Washington family. Her pleading fell on deaf ears, and she decided to return to the city the next day. She just missed the steamboat going up river, and it was necessary to go

Ann Pamela Cunningham

back and spend another night at Mount Vernon. Naturally, she renewed her efforts to win the good will of John Washington, and at last she was successful. Apparently Washington had assumed that the activities of the Mount Vernon Ladies' Association had been one more part of the great public outcry against him. No doubt many Americans were angered by the "unfair" price that he had put upon his home. Ann Pamela assured him that she and her helpers sincerely regretted any unpleasantness that their activities had caused. She went on to say that when the Ladies' Association had been chartered by the Virginia legislature, the charter had not been worked out according to the terms that John Washington had set down. She had tried to get legal help in making the charter more acceptable because she had never wanted to embarrass or trouble the owner of Mount Vernon. Washington melted before her earnest pleas once he realized that her dedication to Mount Vernon was sincere.

One major task remained—and again the abilities of Ann Pamela Cunningham came to the fore. She had to organize and lead the Mount Vernon Ladies' Association through the campaign to raise the $200,000 necessary to purchase the farm. Edward Everett had given a great deal of time and money, but the women of the nation had to do their part. In 1858, Miss Cunningham succeeded in writing a charter for her association that satisfied both John Washington and the Virginia legislature; now she could turn to the problem of winning the support of the American public. There is no question that some people in influential positions were convinced that Americans should not be asked to donate to a fund that would enrich John Washington, and a few editors argued that George Washington's greatness would endure whether or not Mount Vernon was open to the public.

Miss Cunningham now appointed vice-regents for thirty states. At first, she attempted to locate women who were noted for their wealth or fame, but she gradually turned more to ladies who were dedicated to the preservation of Mount Vernon above all else. Each of the vice-regents appointed "lady-managers" (a nicer title than "agent") in each town or county. The lady-managers forwarded subscription lists to the vice-regent who then published the names of contributors to the Mount Vernon fund. Ann Pamela Cunningham told her vice-regents to be sure to enlist the help of "zealous editors" in order to spread the good word about the association. She was quite satisfied with the help of the southern editors, but she found that north of Philadelphia most newspapers did not choose to print long lists of donors or other news of the Mount Vernon campaign. Again Miss Cunningham's regard for George Washington's memory overcame her feminine desire to remain in the background. She helped several friends to establish a newspaper just for the association, and she named it the *Mount Vernon Record*. Although the *Record* only appeared for two years, it fulfilled its particular mission in every respect. One can find in its pages accounts of Mount Vernon meetings all over the country, biographical details on George Washington, and, of course, lists of people who had given money to help purchase Mount Vernon.

Not long before the election of 1860, the *Mount Vernon Record* carried the announcement that the Ladies' Association had been waiting for: the $200,000 had been raised! No matter how much credit is given to Edward Everett and the more faithful vice-regents, it is obvious that the task might never have been accomplished had it not been for the driving energy of an invalid who refused to let the Victorian image of woman's subordinate position govern her actions. If we may believe the accounts of suffering contained in her letters from this period, we can assume that Ann Pamela Cunningham won her victory at a great personal cost. There is no question that she looked upon the campaign to save George Washington's home as more than

Ann Pamela Cunningham

a matter of saving some ancient timbers on a Virginia hilltop, for only a powerful ideal could have driven a southern lady into the glare of the public press.

Miss Cunningham's letters and appeals, written throughout the decade of the 1850's, make it abundantly clear that she saw in her association of women a real hope for American democracy in its darkest hour. In the *Mount Vernon Record* for July, 1858, she warned that the "counsels" of men such as George Washington could "maintain our Union in safety," and then she stated that only "the heart of woman" had responded to the critical need. Furthermore, her letters to Edward Everett in the late 1850's contain references to sectional strife as an evil—while the Mount Vernon Ladies' Association of *the Union* is described as a "beacon light" in the darkness. The only logical conclusion seems to be that both Everett and Miss Cunningham hoped to keep the country out of the Civil War by focusing attention on the virtues symbolized by the home and grave of the first President of the United States.

It would be easy to say that Miss Cunningham must have considered her sacrifice a vain one, because she had to spend the war years at Rosemont in South Carolina—many miles from her beloved association and Mount Vernon. But a brighter day dawned for both Rosemont and the Ladies' Association once the Civil War had ended. To begin with, Ann Pamela returned to take up her duties as Regent in residence at Mount Vernon. This meant that no permanent caretaker would have to be paid while the house was being repaired.

Once she had settled in Mount Vernon, Miss Cunningham's bravery and determination prompted her to enter the grim world of politics one more time. During the entire period of the war, the association had lost its major source of income when the Union Army confiscated the boat that carried tourists to Mount Vernon. The only sensible course of action in 1866 seemed to be to get a bill through Congress granting the Ladies'

Keepers of the Past

Association funds to repair the estate. Miss Cunningham's letters from this period contain even more references to her illnesses, but she went to Washington day after day to plead with senators and representatives who might be sympathetic with her ideals. On many occasions, she had to deal with men such as Charles Sumner, the arch-enemy of South Carolina during the years before the Civil War. Finally, in 1869, Congress did award the association enough money to carry out some important repairs on the mansion, and Mount Vernon appeared to be secure again.

Ann Pamela Cunningham's vision of Mount Vernon was quite specific: it had to be kept as the "home of Washington," and her successors were to be sure not to let "vandal hands desecrate it." Throughout her twenty years as the first Regent of the association, she set a remarkable example as a conservative restorer. It is hard to imagine what we might see today at Mount Vernon had she not been so eager to maintain the atmosphere of the eighteenth century. Some well-meaning patriots asked her to assist them in turning the gardens into a pantheon where American heroes could be memorialized with great statues. One man proposed a "protective" scheme for tearing the house down and then rebuilding it inside a larger marble Mount Vernon. In every case, Miss Cunningham refused to do anything except repair the main structure where it seemed to be weak. She also began to search for original furnishings to restore the interior. The Lee Family helped her many times in the early years as many personal possessions of Washington's had come by inheritance to Mrs. Robert E. Lee. General Lee's son presented the association with Washington's bed and several other items. It would be ridiculous to imply that by 1874, when Ann Pamela Cunningham retired as Regent, Mount Vernon had been successfully restored to its 1799 appearance. Only in recent years have the officials of the Mount Vernon Ladies' Association been able to present to the public the mansion as Washington had seen it. The important fact is that Miss Cunningham started the association in the right direction, and she made surprisingly few mistakes.

Miss Cunningham was more than a preservationist; she was a pioneer in the field of women's rights. It is true that her writings contain little comment on the position of women in a man's society, nor did she discuss female suffrage. Instead, she was the actual founder of the women's patriotic movement that bore rich fruit at the end of the nineteenth century, when a number of patriotic hereditary organizations came into existence all over the United States. Ann Pamela Cunningham had begun her work with her relatives and acquaintances in the South, but she finally had to reach out across the country to find eager and capable workers. The idealism of the Mount Vernon campaign filtered down to the lady-managers who worked on the county level. Some of these women later wrote that they were amazed to see themselves meeting and passing resolutions "just like men" for the first time! By her example, Miss Cunningham proved that a woman *could* found and lead a national organization made up exclusively of women. More than that, she showed that such an association could be successful in a huge undertaking. Even today, the officers and employees of the Mount Vernon Ladies' Association take pride in the fact that they have not deviated from the guidelines set down in Ann Pamela Cunningham's farewell address to the vice-regents in 1874.

Miss Cunningham returned to Rosemont for a well-deserved rest in 1874, but she lived only a few months into the next year. Her passing, however, did not in any way upset her association. Her organizational ability, her writings, and her dedicated successors insured continued progress for the Mount Vernon Ladies.

It would be only fair to list at this point the qualities that were present in this extraordinary woman. She possessed considerable wealth at the beginning of her career, and she had received an excellent education for a woman. There is no question that she had developed courage in facing the ravages of invalidism during the years following her fall from a horse. She expressed herself with ease both as a writer and as a conversationalist. Her letters lead us to believe that she was a mixture of grim determination and deep sincerity. No doubt she could never have won the allegiance of Edward Everett or the friendship of John Washington without such qualities. She must have had a commanding presence that enabled her to work successfully with her talented followers. In a few instances, she was impatient with those that she considered disloyal, but her achievements as an executive were remarkable. There seems to be no hint of selfishness in her nature, and this led her to give herself to a cause rather than to a life of comparative ease. The sacrifice she made was certainly an example to those who worked with her. She was an astute observer of her time, as can be seen by the fact that she fully grasped the nature of the sectional dispute that was leading toward the Civil War—and she hoped to avoid its consequences by a renewed sense of dedication to the Union. She also understood the corruption of the reconstruction years when many Americans were tempted to forget their national heritage in their haste to become rich. Again her answer was one of renewed idealism. Miss Cunningham believed that the women of America were well-equipped to show the leaders of the United States where they should be moving. There is no word in common use that is harder to define than "patriotism," yet we can look back over the career of Ann Pamela Cunningham and conclude that she was in every sense of the word a true patriot.

NOTES

1. Ann Pamela Cunningham, "To the Ladies of the South," *Charleston Mercury*, Dec. 2, 1853, Early Records I, p. 1, Archives of the Mount Vernon Ladies' Association of the Union, Mount Vernon, Virginia.

2. Edward Everett, *Journal*, quoted in Paul Revere Frothingham, *Edward Everett, Orator and Statesman* (Boston, 1925), p. 377.

Adina De Zavala

by L. Robert Ables

Be sure you're right,
then go ahead[1]

David Crockett's famous aphorism has stood as a staunch guidepost for many, but it has served no one better than Adina De Zavala[2] of San Antonio, who devoted most of her ninety-three years to discovering and preserving Texas history. How do you "discover and preserve" history? It *can* be done, as Miss De Zavala clearly demonstrated during her active life.

Perceiving that many historic structures in Texas were being lost forever, Miss De Zavala took steps to recover, to rededicate. She determined that students in the future should not only read the history of Texas but view it as well. Although she sometimes met defeat, she never deviated from her purpose, and those with whom she came in contact always knew they had dealt with Adina De Zavala.

Miss De Zavala, born in 1861, grew to womanhood under the shadow of her illustrious grandfather, Lorenzo de Zavala, who took the side of Texans against Santa Anna and became the first vice president of the new republic. After attending Catholic schools during her earlier life, Miss De Zavala enrolled at Sam

Houston Normal Institute at Huntsville, Texas, in 1879; taught school at Terrell, Texas, and later at San Antonio.

In one of her displays of initiative, she attended a San Antonio school board meeting Nov. 5, 1900, and presented a letter protesting her low salary. The letter was read aloud at the meeting, and Miss De Zavala, typically, must have pressed her point strongly. The only result evidenced by the minutes is that the board passed a motion stating that teachers must submit their complaints in writing "as they will not be allowed to come before the board to make verbal complaints."

In 1902, the board voted to notify Miss De Zavala that if she did not sign her teacher contract immediately, a substitute would be named. She signed, but two months later she protested to the board again that she was entitled to a higher salary.

The following year, she employed a novel method of collecting a debt—if, indeed, it may be called a debt. The board voted that a Mrs. Clint Campbell should be informed that nothing could be done about her claim that Miss De Zavala owed a board bill. The grievance committee quoted Miss De Zavala as saying that Mrs. Campbell had rented a house from Miss De Zavala's mother and carried off fixtures. Miss De Zavala ". . . after deducting her board bill . . . had it figured out that Mrs. Campbell was in debt to her in the sum of $2.40."

Miss De Zavala's character and personality cast her well as organizer and leader of historical groups. As early as 1889, she began meeting with a few women friends "to keep green the memory of the heroes."[3] In 1893, this San Antonio group was incorporated as the De Zavala Chapter of the Daughters of the Republic of Texas (DRT), a woman's organization composed of descendants of early Texans. One of the first projects of the De Zavala Chapter was to mark with a monument the grave of Ben Milam, who was killed in 1835 during the capture of San Antonio from the Mexican army. The women chose March 6, the day the Alamo fell in 1836, as Texas Heroes Day,

Adina De Zavala

and conducted commemorative exercises at the graveside of Milam for the first time in 1897.

The women also sought to "save" the missions which had fallen into various states of disrepair, including the famous Alamo in the heart of San Antonio.

The original "Alamo,"[4] as the world today terms it, was established in 1718 and named San Antonio de Valero. The mission consisted of a long two-story building—variously referred to as the convent, monastery, long barrack, or fortress. A chapel, which is extant and the "Alamo" of today, later was erected a few yards from the fortress, and the mission area was surrounded by a wall, along parts of which shelters were built. Before 1836, the roof of the chapel collapsed and debris limited the usefulness of the old building. The Texans only temporarily defended the outer walls of the mission against Santa Anna, and most of them retired to the more compact and better defensive position of the long barrack. The major portion of the struggle took place in and around this fortress.

In 1883, the State of Texas bought the chapel from the Catholic church, and by the turn of the century, a wholesale grocery firm, Hugo and Schmeltzer, owned the remnants of the fortress portion. Adjacent real estate also was in private hands.

Nearly everyone desired to preserve the Alamo, but exactly what constituted the crumbling mission and how preservation should be accomplished were open to dispute. After considerable confusion during the early years, arguments gradually were polarized with one group following Mrs. Hal Sevier, better known by her maiden name of Clara Driscoll, a vivacious and rich leader of Texas women, and another group supporting Miss De Zavala. An article by Tom Finty, Jr., in the Dallas *Morning News,* December 31, 1911, summarizes the situation at that date:

> One faction ... led by Miss De Zavala, has contended that the walls of the Hugo & Schmeltzer Building are original

parts of the building in which the defenders of the Alamo made their last stand.... They assert that these walls should be preserved and the building restored.

The other faction, led by Miss Clara Driscoll ... contends that the Hugo & Schmeltzer Building is not historically sacred; that of its wall only eight feet was a part of the Alamo, and that was simply a wall inclosing the grounds of the monastery, whereas the monastery itself was further back. They would tear all of this building down ... and leave only the jagged remains of the eight-foot wall. They would make the grounds into a park and erect upon it a monument to the heroes ... they contend that the Alamo Chapel is the real Alamo.

Eight years earlier, in 1903, the two women had been allies. Miss Driscoll, after studying in Europe, had returned to Texas and joined the De Zavala Chapter of the DRT. Pompeo Coppini, an Italian sculptor who had moved to San Antonio in 1901, reported the first contact Miss De Zavala had with Miss Driscoll. Commercial interests planned to buy the Hugo and Schmeltzer building and offered Coppini the commission for a ten-foot statue of Crockett to be placed in the foyer of a hotel proposed for the site. Coppini was aghast at the idea of commercializing the "sacred" ground: "... I made a beeline for Miss Adina De Zavala's home ... I knew of all she was doing ... for since I had become interested in Texas history, she had been my inspiring educator.... Miss Adina and Lizzie [Coppini's wife] went out every day with our horse and buggy ... for ... contributions of bricks, lumber, cedar posts, or wire to repair ... all the missions, the chapel of the Alamo included."[5]

Miss De Zavala and Coppini laid plans to thwart the proposed purchase and decided to visit the Kampmanns, owners of the Menger Hotel, who would be interested not only in saving the Alamo grounds but, at the same time, in eliminating

Adina De Zavala

competition for the Menger. They found that the Kampmann family was in Paris, but Mrs. Kampmann's sister, Mrs. George E. Eichlitz, remembered that a "very prominent, rich and very ambitious young woman who may be of some help" was at the hotel. Her name was Clara Driscoll.

The two talked to Miss Driscoll, with Coppini picturing "what it would mean to make reality the dream of the De Zavala Chapter of the Daughters of the Republic of Texas to preserve as a shrine one of the most sacred of all spots," and: "Before Miss Adina and I left the hotel, we had good reason to believe that we had prevented the Hugo & Schmeltzer Building from falling into the hands of the Eastern syndicate. . . ."

The three female principals involved in the fortuitous event impressed Coppini, and his mind may have wandered to his youthful days in Europe as he wrote: "I thought the combination was a good omen. Miss Adina was a . . . genteel Spanish type; Mrs. Eichlitz had the sculpturesque features and figure of a real Germania; and Miss Driscoll was a feminine . . . fiery . . . Irish type, a commanding beauty."

Miss De Zavala was small—about five feet three inches tall—during her young womanhood. She had soft brown hair, but "the Spanish stopped at the blue eyes," which likely came from the Irish side of her family. Coppini, recalling the first time he saw Miss De Zavala, described her as "an exceptionally beautiful woman. . . . She carried herself with dignity but also with a gentleness of manner. . . ."

One of her close friends later in life, Miss Frances Donecker of San Antonio, likened her to a self-reliant "Spanish grandmother, small of stature but firm of character." And as Miss De Zavala's years increased, she good-naturedly refused to reveal their sum. Her physician once inquired if he might ask her age. She smiled and answered, "You may, but you won't get a reply."

In March, 1903, Miss Driscoll gave her personal check for $500 to the Hugo and Schmeltzer interests for an option on the property, which the owners agreed to sell to the Daughters for $75,000. The De Zavala Chapter was to pay $4,500 more within thirty days, and the option was to be extended to February 10, 1904. Miss Driscoll also wrote this second check. In the meantime, the Daughters launched a public campaign to "save" the Alamo, but less than $6,000 was donated. Miss Driscoll again stepped into the breach by adding, from her personal fortune, more than $14,000 to satisfy the required down payment of $25,000, and she signed notes for the remaining $50,000 due the Hugo and Schmeltzer interests.

With fingers on the public pulse and at the constant prodding of the Daughters, the Texas legislature, in January, 1905, voted to purchase the Hugo and Schmeltzer building and award custody to the DRT. The state now owned both the chapel and the fortress area, and the courageous Miss Driscoll recouped her risky financial outlay.

Shortly thereafter, persistent internal differences began to plague the DRT organization. Miss De Zavala considered that her San Antonio chapter should be the *de facto* custodian, but the executive committee, a sort of board of directors for the DRT, appointed Miss Driscoll temporary custodian. Miss Driscoll named a friend to keep the Alamo open for the public, and soon the Daughters found themselves engaged in a catastrophic controversy over custodianship of the old mission, over preservation, and over control of the DRT organization.

Adding fuel to the flames, in 1906, was a letter received by Miss De Zavala from Charles M. Reeves of St. Louis. Reeves informed her that, as representative of St. Louis hotel interests, he had bought property adjoining the Alamo, and with "proper encouragement" by the DRT, a "splendid structure" would be erected. Before building the hotel, however, he desired assurance that the Hugo and Schmeltzer "warehouse" would be torn down and the grounds converted into a park. He added that, when he was in San Antonio, he was informed that the state or the DRT had agreed to do so.

In her reply, Miss De Zavala explained that the walls of the building occupied by Hugo and Schmeltzer was the Alamo proper and that the church was the chapel of the Alamo. She outlined her plans to remove everything modern and restore the fortress as a "Hall of Fame" with the second floor to house an "art gallery" with a glass roof.

Reeves did not realize that his next letter unfurled the blood-red banner of no quarter—just as had Santa Anna seventy years earlier. He explained that her plan was impractical and "can only result in disappointment to yourself and the noble women. . . ." The Alamo should stand, he said, but "At the time of the battle of the Alamo only the South wall of the Mission was standing. Texas patriots wish to preserve only that which has to do with . . . history. . . . What you propose to do in the perpetuation of the walls of this old building would simply result in preserving indefinitely an eye-sore. . . . No business man is going to allow his better judgment to be swayed by a misguided sense of patriotism. . . ."[6]

The factional split in the DRT organization, already pronounced, grew worse. Custodianship became crucial in the face of this renewed threat of commercial intrusion.

Miss De Zavala and her group went to the annual state convention of the DRT in April, 1907, at Austin, and in a tumultuous session, her opponents—the Driscoll group—adjourned the meeting *sine die*. The De Zavala faction promptly elected a rival slate of state officers and named Miss De Zavala chairman of the new executive committee. The new officers declared themselves the heads of the state organization and began carrying out the functions of such offices. Three months later, the regular executive committee was granted an injunction against the De Zavala group, which was ordered to cease its interfering tactics until rightful officers could be determined by the courts.

Keepers of the Past

The regular executive committee group, the plaintiff, later filed a supplemental petition stating in part:

> The public at large do not understand that the major portion of the ground which was originally purchased by Miss Clara Driscoll from Hugo & Schmeltzer . . . is not occupied by any portion of the original Alamo building or mission, but that same is occupied by a building erected long after the fall of the Alamo. . . . That many people not familiar with the facts believe . . . that this building is a part of the building that was hallowed by the blood of heroes of Texas, when in truth and in fact it has never been hallowed except by good, bad and indifferent whisky. It was the intention of plaintiff's Executive Committee . . . to remove this unsightly building and place in lieu thereof either a park, museum or something else.

With the issue still before the courts, an event occurred that received national newspaper coverage and put the name of Adina De Zavala on the lips of thousands, perhaps millions. A lease, granted to the Hugo and Schmeltzer interests after the state bought the property, was to expire February 10, 1908. Miss De Zavala entered the Hugo and Schmeltzer building in the late afternoon or early evening of the tenth, barricaded herself inside, and refused to leave for three days. She later wrote that she ". . . had learned on good authority that a syndicate which had an option upon the property back of the Alamo intended to seize the Alamo and tear it down, so as to use the space as part of the Plaza, a sort of front yard to the Hotel. . . ."

Sheriff John Tobin and others went to the Alamo grounds armed with an injunction, ordering Miss De Zavala to cease interference until litigation with the DRT was settled. The San Antonio *Light* reported that: "An attempt was made to serve the injunction upon Miss De Zavala by the sheriff, but the decrees of the court brought no fear. . . . She refused to accept

Adina De Zavala

a copy of the document and when an attempt was made to read it to her she stopped her ears with her fingers."

The embroilment was resolved quickly as the women and their attorneys agreed that the state should intervene. Miss De Zavala surrendered the property to W. C. Day, state superintendent of public buildings, February 13.

The *Light,* probably without too much exaggeration for the times, said the controversy ". . . has heretofore torn Texas from Texarkana to El Paso—and from where the Rio Grande winds its way to the muddy banks of the Red River. . . . Erstwhile friends have become sworn enemies—and those who formerly drank tea and exchanged small talk together . . . are arrayed . . . in a warfare quite as determined as the defense of the Alamo in 1836. . . ."

Words and actions from both sides kept the caldron boiling until, eventually, Governor Oscar Colquitt stepped into the arena. A meeting was called for December 28, 1911, to give the governor the facts. Finty, the Dallas *Morning News* reporter, told his readers that the Driscoll group said the U.S. Army had erected the Hugo and Schmeltzer building after the annexation of Texas by the United States. The governor stated that he thought none of the Alamo that antedated its fall should be torn away, that a park or monument could not take the place of the original Alamo as a shrine, and that no part should be used for commercial profit.

Miss De Zavala presented her historical case, which included an unpublished plat of the Alamo at the time of its fall, and Governor Colquitt asked her to send the material to him.

Miss Driscoll arrived at the meeting a few minutes late and missed some of the points made by the governor. He repeated the substance of his remarks for her, and she replied, "I have never sanctioned touching one of the original stones; but I don't think the Alamo should be disgraced by this whisky house, which obscures the most remarkable relic of the world."

Keepers of the Past

At another point in the meeting, Finty stated that "H. P. Drought read a communication from Mrs. Rebecca Fisher [president of the Daughters of the Republic] ... and the other officers and executive committee of that association, asking the governor to sanction their plan for tearing down the Hugo & Schmeltzer building and for parking of the grounds."

The meeting itself settled little or nothing, with both sides holding tenaciously to their views. Later, Governor Colquitt began to restore the fortress, but the task was never completed.

The district court meanwhile had ruled that the regular Daughters group constituted the legal officers of the DRT. Miss De Zavala and other defendants appealed, but the higher courts affirmed the previous judgment. The Alamo property was turned over formally to the victorious group of Daughters on March 10, 1910. As far as the now court-sanctioned DRT was concerned, the De Zavala Chapter was out of existence, and "these individuals could no longer claim to be members of the organization ... nor in any way use this name to sponsor their actions...." Thus, Miss De Zavala completely lost her court fight and any part of the custodianship of the Alamo grounds and control of the DRT. Nevertheless, she fruitlessly fought for restoration, practically to her deathbed, and of the many projects she undertook in her long life, it is ironic that one of the earliest and most grandiose was not totally successful. Time illuminated her historical acumen, however, for most of her contentions concerning the Alamo have proved to be correct, and if she ever thought of retiring from the field of battle during her fifty-year crusade, she probably recalled the sentence she wrote after barricading herself in the Alamo in 1908: "... you know Davy Crockett ... said, 'Be sure you're right, then go ahead.'"

Having lost her fight to control the DRT, Miss De Zavala now set up her own organization. In 1912, she formed the Texas Historical and Landmarks Association, dedicated to preserving historic sites in Texas. By now, she was indeed a formidable

Adina De Zavala

person. One of her colleagues and admirers of this period later recalled: "... her frail body had the strength of a giant. Once having a selected objective, she remained on the trail until it could be marked accomplished. At times, she was a martinet. For instance, at one meeting of the Association, the question of the election of officers came up. She solved it by pointing ... and saying, 'You are President'; and then pointing ... and saying, 'You are the Vice-President'."

As early as 1915, an ancient stone edifice in San Antonio caught her eye. A coat of arms above the door first stirred her interest, and finally, after assiduous pursuit of archival material, she discovered that the neglected old eyesore was none other than the Spanish Governor's Palace, the seat of the royal government of Spain in Texas after the 1730's.

As soon as Miss De Zavala realized the historical significance of the palace, which was fast tumbling into ruin, she opened a campaign to restore it as a museum. In 1919, she became editor of a San Antonio magazine reporting industrial activities of the area, but she quickly converted the owner—and the magazine—to the cause of Texas history and saving the Governor's Palace. By 1928, public interest in the preservation of the palace was such that the city purchased it for $55,000 and spent an additional $30,000 restoring it.

Miss De Zavala achieved another historical triumph, appropriately enough, during the Texas centennial in 1936. Members of the De Zavala historical groups had for years honored a site near the altar railing of San Fernando Cathedral in San Antonio as the burial place of several Alamo defenders after their bodies were burned on orders of Santa Anna in 1836. Miss De Zavala based her contention principally on a letter written in 1889 by Juan Seguin, a responsible Texas patriot, who said that he buried the remains in the church. The historical enigma was not solved until workmen, excavating for a new altar foundation, uncovered charred human bones July 28, 1936. Historians and

Keepers of the Past

interested persons agreed that the remains unearthed were those of Alamo defenders.

The years slipped by, and as all things at last must end, so did Miss De Zavala's tempestuous career. After an injury from a fall, she died March 1, 1955, a few hours before the dawn of her beloved Texas Independence Day. The funeral was held March 5, and the *Southern Messenger,* a San Antonio Catholic weekly, reported: "Her casket was draped with the Texas Flag.... On its way to St. Mary's cemetery...the funeral procession passed by the historic Alamo in final tribute to Miss De Zavala who had so valiantly defended the Shrine of Texas Liberty, and was instrumental in keeping it from being sold to hotel interests shortly after the turn of the century."

SOURCES AND NOTES

The major source is The Adina De Zavala Papers, The University of Texas Library Archives, Austin. The personal library of Miss Frances Donecker of San Antonio contains considerable material concerning Miss De Zavala's life. Newspapers from the San Antonio Public Library as well as clippings from the above two collections were utilized. Among specialized sources most of the material on incidents while she was teaching came from *Minutes of the Board of Education of the San Antonio School District,* Vols. A, B, D, and I.

1. Larry Mills in his *The Sayings of Davy Crockett in His Own Language* (Dallas, 1938), states that the actual quote is: "Be always sure you're right, then go ahead."
2. The De Zavala family anglicized its name slightly by capitalizing the *d* in de Zavala.
3. See Miss De Zavala's small book, *History and Legends of the Alamo,* which was reprinted under the title, *The Alamo, Where the Last Man Died* (San Antonio, 1956). She also wrote hundreds of newspaper and magazine articles concerning Texas history.
4. This name was attached to the mission, most historians believe, because the Spanish "Alamo" army company was stationed there in the early nineteenth century.
5. Pompeo Coppini, *From Dawn to Sunset* (San Antonio, 1949).
6. Adina De Zavala Papers, The University of Texas Library Archives, Austin.

William Sumner Appleton

by Bertram K. Little

Early in 1910, a thirty-six-year-old Bostonian evolved an idea and a purpose that resulted in a new organization. With it, he not only pioneered in historic preservation but also helped to open this field to the students of art, architecture, and social history who seek a career calling on all of their interests and abilities. Born behind the purple panes of 39 Beacon Street, one of Boston's (and Massachusetts') finest bow-fronted houses and living there until 1886 may well have contributed to William Sumner Appleton's early interest in art and achitecture. The independence of spirit, judgment, and action that he exercised in quiet, selfless leadership throughout his life's work and the other qualities that Sumner, as this son of William Sumner and Edith Stuart Appleton was always called, possessed—kindliness, patience, frugality—came naturally from his parents, grandparents, and the English ancestors who had settled in Ipswich, Massachusetts, in 1636.

By 1750, a group of these early settlers, feeling the urge to move on to larger landholdings and opportunities, founded New Ipswich, New Hampshire, where, tradition has it, they offered to work the farm of Deacon Isaac Appleton if he would teach their children. In this practical arrangement can be seen the beginning of the Appleton Academy of today. As the eight sons of the deacon grew up, first Samuel, and then Nathan, journeyed regularly to Boston to purchase supplies needed by such rural communities. They were so successful in their trading that, by 1794, the two brothers had formed a partnership and established a warehouse on Boston's Cornhill.

In 1816, Nathan Appleton built the Boston house in which his grandson, Sumner, was born on May 29, 1874, the only boy in a family with four girls. Sumner, never a husky lad, had such a severe case of diphtheria in his late teens that he had to take his college entrance examinations in a wheel chair. At the impressionable age of thirteen, he had the eye-and-mind-opening experience of living more than a year abroad with his entire family.

A series of twenty-four closely packed scrapbooks vividly reveals Sumner Appleton's social activities and developing interests during his undergraduate years at Harvard, 1892-96, and on through the first decade of the new century when he studied at the University's Bussey Institution, 1905-6, and at its Graduate School of Arts and Sciences, 1906-7, with emphasis on American architecture. For example, in 1893, besides receiving formal notice of his membership in the Saturday Evening Dancing Class, he chose to attend a performance in Eleanora Duse's first American tour, see Julia Marlowe in *The Love Chase* at the Hollis Street Theatre, hear concerts by Paderewski, and enjoy Damrosch conducting the New York Symphony Orchestra in the Music Hall. He attended the World's Columbian Exposition at Chicago that year and the United States National Lawn Tennis Tournament at Newport Casino the next.

Then during the summer and fall following the receipt of his A.B. degree, Appleton made the "Grand Tour" of Europe with his former tutor. In 1898, he formed a real estate firm with Lombard Williams and was actively engaged in it some three years, often seeking to interest clients in houses and buildings of an earlier day. Continuing ill health forced him to dissolve the firm, and several years passed before he was able to work again. In the meantime, three sisters married and his father died, leaving his fortune in trust for his offspring, which prevented Sumner from entering any business requiring the investment of capital. This circumstance produced unforeseen but fortunate results.

Work on a volunteer committee to save the Paul Revere House in Boston was perhaps the catalyst that, bringing into focus Appleton's earlier thinking and observation and his consciously selected educational and business experience, produced the idea of forming the Society for the Preservation of New England Antiquities. Before the founding of this society no organized effort had been made, in New England or elsewhere in the United States, on a multiple-state regional basis, to preserve ancient buildings and other examples of the domestic arts and crafts *as a related whole.*

Appleton's large and flowing script makes the entries in his "line-a-day" diary even more telegraphic in style than usual, but they nonetheless reveal something of the incessant work he put into the development of every element in his concept of the society and the natural excitement of accomplishment. On January 4, 1910, his first entry on the matter states, "Had long talk with C. K. Bolton [who became the first president] about starting a Society for the Preservation of New England Antiquities; looks like a go. Talked with Joe Minot, who thought it impracticable." The following day he was "chatting" with several other men "on S.P.N.E.A.," receiving "some encouragement." Subsequent entries exult in enlisting, one by one, the seventeen men and women who became with him incorporators of the society; reflect the care and time spent on drawing up the charter and bylaws of the new organization and designing its seal; and record his successful personal following of the special act creating the Society through the whole legislative process.

Keepers of the Past

On April 23, appears the triumphal entry: "10:30 A.M. in the Council Room of N.E.H.G.S., incorporators' meeting of the S.P.N.E.A. Then 1st Director's meeting. All went well!" By April 27, he was working "all day on the circular and 1st Bulletin for the S.P.N.E.A.," but on May 3, he notes that the Committee on Increase of Membership "hashed up my circular." However, the seal of the society was ordered the next day, and the society now was most definitely in the business of safeguarding New England's architectural heritage.

If, as the old saying goes, the first hundred years are the hardest, then perhaps the first ten of this society might be comparable. A brief review of the first ten of the thirty-seven annual reports that Sumner Appleton wrote as the society's corresponding secretary—for he declined any other title except the later addition of manager of real estate—will show more clearly than anything the fullness of the criteria, standards, practicalities, and principles he set for the Preservation Society. His diary, it is true, sets forth a number of practicalities, such as the equal use of the interest and abilities of men and women as trustees, the limitation of their terms, and the development of an unusual volunteer custodian system that has proved perhaps the greatest single factor in making manageable the increased number of houses under the society's control; but it is his annual reports and correspondence that reveal the full power and originality of Appleton's thinking and action which have so deeply influenced the practice of historic preservation.

The reports record Appleton's pioneering development of an ever-expanding collection, filed geographically, of new England photographs and negatives, post cards, stereoscopic views, clippings, pamphlets, and every sort of historical ephemera. They underline his insistence on the recording, by measurement, photograph, and written notes, of every house or building that met the criteria of architectural and historical importance. They originate certain standards in the accomplishing of preservation or restoration work. Appleton formulated three prime essentials: (1) the preliminary painstaking exploration of existing evidence and conditions; (2) the abstention from conjectural restoration if later changes were interesting in themselves and earlier features could be interpreted through them; and (3) the documentation of every action taken during restoration and subsequent maintenance. The reports also demonstrate the society's policies of attempting to preserve the best houses of each type, to spread the realization of the importance of historic preservation by accepting properties throughout its six-state area, and to aid in every possible way the preservation efforts of others, both individuals and organizations.

It was a great day for Sumner when a member presented an Ediphone to the society. It enabled him to lay aside his pince-nez glasses, drape his six-foot-plus, well-proportioned form over an armchair in his headquarters office and dictate letters at night, on Sundays, and on holidays. These letters should someday be edited, because they contain a wealth of helpful advice concerning work on preservation projects and a real insight into the motivation of volunteers and professionals alike. They show his tactfulness in handling trustees, members, and custodians—making each one feel Appleton recognized how personally and helpfully he was a part of the society's success. In a letter to a long-time member, written, he explains, only at the insistence of the treasurer because she had failed to pay two years' dues, he gives her the choice of continuing to help the society by remitting the dues or of having him send her a complimentary membership ticket so that her "senior standing" may be maintained until she finds it convenient to become a paying member again. In another, he describes a visit to an old Connecticut house with the eminent architect Fred Kelly where they found some good panelling and many flea-bitten cats. On leaving, they sought the bushes at the edge of a neighboring pasture and considered it lucky that there were no visitors around to see two architectural historians, stripped down as far as the law allowed, ridding each other of fleas.

The late seventeenth-century Abraham Browne House in Watertown, Massachusetts, may well be considered Appleton's outstanding monument. Saved from near collapse in 1919, because, as he writes, "I got mad and decided it shouldn't be pulled down," he directed its restoration and described the process in the most thorough day-by-day records of any restoration in New England. Early in the course of the project, he wrote to a friend: "The work...is now well under way and you and Mr. Isham are both worrying for fear I may be destroying evidence as I go along.... I am, in spite of the criticism that I get, the most conservative restorer...and a building is in the safest hands when I have charge of it." This was a boast he could honestly make, but it should be noted that he adds: "Kindly observe my modesty!" Appleton wrote copious letters to, and sometimes became a member of, many organizations in England and on the Continent, including those with such intriguing titles as the Society for the Preservation of Commons, Footpaths and Open Spaces, and the Society for the Preservation of Windmills in the Netherlands, which served not only to keep him closely in touch with the work and practice of historic preservation abroad but also to make the Society for the Preservation of New England Antiquities known internationally. His abilities as an editor are apparent through even a cursory glance at the 118 issues of the society's *Bulletin* (later *Old-Time New England*), which he personally guided to press and for which he wrote many articles in addition to his annual reports.

Although he volunteered innumerable hours to the affairs of the society and contributed both objects and funds, Sumner Appleton kept up the interests reflected earlier in his scrapbooks—art, music, and the theater. He generously invited friends and members of the society's staff to enjoy them with him, and this perennial bachelor was often seen in the company of young ladies who addressed him affectionately as "Uncle Sumner"—and, indeed, he was related to many a Boston family. He never lost his enthusiasm for football, always holding season tickets for the Harvard games. He loved to spend completely relaxed weeks at Nantucket, with an occasional few days on the antiquarian road, and had an uncanny way with trains that conveniently landed him in various parts of New England where friends could meet him and whirl him by car to more out-of-the-way points.

Two signal awards were made to Appleton during his lifetime: the first, in 1944, when the Trustees of Reservations presented him their reward for Distinguished Service for Conservation; and the second, in 1946, when he received the George McAneny medal of the American Scenic and Historic Preservation Society with the following citation:

> William Sumner Appleton: By birth, instinct, preference and profession a New Englander, you have been a diligent preserver in tangible form of the traditions, the manners and customs and the ancient habitations of New England. To that end you have given the substance of your heart, frame and wallet. You yourself have become a tradition as a fervid, fearless fighter for the faith that is in you. That faith is embodied in the Society for the Preservation of New England Antiquities, and you have been its modest mentor and mainspring for almost forty years of struggle against inertia, indifference and greed. You have met success and frustration with an even mind, but victory for preservation has been so often on your side that historians of the nation revere you.

At its thirtieth annual meeting, the society he had founded paid deserved tribute to Sumner: first, by acknowledging that his wisdom and tireless zeal had caused the growth of the society in membership from eighteen incorporators to over two thousand, and in property from a rented half-office to ownership of over forty historic houses, thousands of interesting and valuable antiquities in those houses, and more in the society's New England Museum; and second, by naming the auditorium on the ground floor of the Harrison Gray Otis house, Appleton Hall. While this hall in the society's headquarters bore his name, it was characteristic of the man that he could only see it as sorely needed additional space for taking care of the mass of material he gathered for the society's collections. It was not until after his death in Lawrence, Massachusetts, on November 24, 1947, following a severe stroke suffered during a field study trip of old vehicles and houses eleven days earlier, that it could be transformed into a real memorial to his wealth of knowledge and valiant service in antiquarian research and to the historic preservation that he proved could be a challenging and worthwhile field of human endeavor.

SOURCES

The sources are the letters, reports, minutes of meetings, notes, and memoranda in the files of the Society for the Preservation of New England Antiquities, Boston, during the period of Appleton's directorship.

Stephen Hyatt Pelham Pell

by Edward P. Hamilton

Stephen Hyatt Pelham Pell, eighth in descent from Thomas Pell (1613-69), first Lord of Pelham Manor, was born in Flushing, Long Island, February 3, 1874, one of several children of John H. Pell and Caroline Hyatt. Little is known of his early years beyond the fact that he was educated at the Flushing Institute and that his father died when he was quite young. Shortly after he left school, he visited the West—in those days still largely untamed—and tried his hand at ranching in Texas. In 1894, he was working for a firm in Wall Street, probably in connection with real estate rather than the stock market. The previous year he had joined the New York Naval Militia, a connection he maintained for seven years. In 1895-96, he made a leisurely trip around the world as secretary to a man of wealth.

Pell's first great adventure came when, along with the rest of the naval militia, he volunteered for service in the Spanish American War and was assigned to the auxiliary cruiser *Yankee*. Almost the entire crew of this converted merchantman came from the naval militia, and it was a congenial crowd of young professionals and men-about-town. The transition from their civilian occupations to that of common sailors was a major one, indeed, but they all appear to have taken up their new life with spirit and enthusiasm. Stephen was assigned as gun captain of one of the light six pounders on the gun deck, and he proceeded to enjoy himself despite weevily corn meal and maggoty biscuits. He kept an amusing diary of his experiences on the *Yankee*. As the war broke out, he appears to have been courting, probably not too seriously, a young lady named "B———," and he spent many an evening with her before the *Yankee* sailed south to Cuban waters. When a letter arrived saying that she had married someone else, his diary cheerfully remarks, "Well, there are others!" The *Yankee* engaged in one or two minor actions and took part in the blockade of Santiago. Then, the war over, she steamed north again, and her crew was released to civil life.

Pell returned to the real-estate business, joining the successful firm of his brother Osgood, and again entered into the life of New York society. An attractive and delightful young man of impeccable social standing, he must have been one of New York's most eligible young bachelors, a state he was not to enjoy for long.

Robert M. Thompson, father of Pell's bride-to-be, graduated from the U.S. Naval Academy in 1868 but soon resigned from the service, then attended the Harvard Law School, was admitted to the Massachusetts Bar, and started practice in Boston. He married Sarah Gibbs, daughter of a former governor of Rhode Island. Thompson, before many years, became involved in copper interests in the West and later was instrumental in forming the International Nickel Co. He soon became a man of great wealth. His only daughter Sarah had gone to school with Pell's sister Mary and the two young people had met from time to time. Late in the summer of 1900, Stephen received an invitation to accompany the Thompson family in their private car for a week's inspection trip of some Canadian mines. By the end of the trip, he and Sarah were engaged, surreptitiously for the moment, for the Thompsons were most jealous of their only child and were not yet ready to lose her. Later, when the news

Stephen Hyatt Pelham Pell

was broken to them, the Thompsons urged delay but soon gave in, and Stephen and Sarah were married in April, 1901. They set up housekeeping at Sands Point, Long Island, and a winter house in New York was soon added.

Shortly after his marriage, Pell was admitted to the New York Stock Exchange and embarked on his career in Wall Street, where the market operations of Thompson and his friends gave him ample business. The young couple now entered into the social life of New York with its rounds of dinners and other activities. Colonel Thompson had an amazing number of friends overseas, and it would seem that whenever a visiting personality hailing from anywhere between England and Japan visited this country he would be entertained by the Thompsons and the Stephen Pells. In short, by 1908, we find Stephen Pell a bright and well-liked ornament of New York Society, a man without the slightest apparent interest in history or the restoration of an ancient structure.

In colonial and revolutionary America, there were few roads in the interior and man moved principally by water. From New York City, the Hudson ascends 150 miles due north to Albany and then on to Fort Edward, where it swings to the west. From Fort Edward, an overland carry of a dozen miles connected with a brook flowing into Lake Champlain, which in turn gave free water access to Canada. Practically all intercourse between Canada and the British colonies had traveled by this route, particularly the military expeditions whose great bulk of provisions, artillery, and munitions could, practically speaking, move only by water. The great waterway from New York to the St. Lawrence was of vital importance during the colonial and revolutionary wars, and he who controlled it held the fate of North America in his hand. In 1755, the French built a fort at Ticonderoga, replacing in importance one previously built a few miles farther north at Crown Point. For a generation, Fort Ticonderoga, called Fort Carillon by the French, was the key to

Keepers of the Past

a continent. Six times armies marched against it in the course of some twenty years; thrice it held and thrice it fell. No fort on this continent, or the entire world, can boast such a record.

In the fall of 1777, the British, staggering back from the debacle of Saratoga, abandoned the old fortress, burning all of the structure that would burn, and retreated to Canada. For years the place stood empty. Then the rush of new settlers, freed at last from all threat of Indian raids, poured into the region and occupied the fertile lands. The old fort and its surrounding grounds remained in the possession of the new State of New York, until they were given to Columbia and Union colleges as a land grant to be sold to help their finances. Meanwhile, the new settlers had found the old walls of the fort an easy stone quarry, and much of the structure had been carried away to build cellar walls and stone houses. The earth behind the upper part of the walls fell and covered the base, and soon only dirt-covered mounds outlined the old fortress.

William Ferris Pell, a New York merchant, while passing up and down Lake Champlain, noted the ruins of the old fort and became enamored of the place. In 1820, he bought the fort and its grounds from the two colleges, and built a summer home. This burned before many years, and in 1826, he built the Pavilion, which stands today, one of America's first summer homes. For years, the Pell family passed their summers at Ticonderoga.

In 1838, the eldest son, who usually remained at Ticonderoga to manage the estate, was killed by the explosion of a cannon with which he was greeting the arrival of the family's boat. The Pells then lost interest in the place. A few years later, William Ferris Pell died, and the ownership of the fort and its grounds was divided among several heirs. By this time, a summer excursion up Lake George, across to Lake Champlain, and then on by steamer to Burlington or farther north to Canada had become fashionable. The Pavilion was leased by the Pells

Stephen Hyatt Pelham Pell

and was operated as a hotel catering to travelers brought overland by stage coach from the foot of Lake George. This arrangement continued for many years, with the family always retaining its ownership, and some of them occasionally were guests at the hotel. Stephen Pell once visited there as a small boy, and, when playing among the ruins of the old fort, he had found a little French tinder box, today one of the prize exhibits in the fort's museum. Toward the end of the century, the Lake George and Champlain trip having lost its old appeal, the hotel went out of business and the Pavilion became a farm house. Throughout the years, however, the descendants of William Ferris Pell retained ownership. The land was held as an undivided interest by a trustee who distributed the rent among the several heirs.

At various times, there had been talk of restoring Fort Ticonderoga, but nothing had resulted. At one time, it was hoped that the federal government would take over the land and rebuild the fort. A bill to that effect was introduced in Congress in 1897 and again in 1906, but all came to naught, and cows continued to amble over the mounds of earth that covered the remains of the old walls.

In 1908, the Ticonderoga Historical Society decided to celebrate the 150th anniversary of the great 1758 battle in which Abercromby hurled his mighty army of 14,000 men against Montcalm's puny force and suffered disastrous defeat. A huge clambake was arranged. Since Stephen Pell was one of the owners of the fort grounds and was reputed to be of great wealth, it is probable that the society invited him to attend the celebration with hope and ulterior motives. He came to Ticonderoga to the clambake, his first visit since as a boy of eight he had found the little tinder box.

There Pell met Alfred Bossom, a young British architect who had come to this country to practice his profession. Today he sits in the House of Peers, Lord Bossom of Maidstone. For some time, he had been doing work in the Adirondacks. He had visited Fort Ticonderoga, had become fascinated with it, and had made some tentative sketches for a possible restoration. When Pell and Bossom met at the clambake, the New York society man quickly succumbed to the idea of rebuilding the old fortress. From that day on, it was to become the major interest of his life.

When Stephen told Sarah Pell of his thoughts on restoring the old ruins, she became even more enthusiastic than he and at once suggested the idea to her father. Colonel Thompson heartily approved, told the Pells to go ahead and to send him the bill. It was a most suitable moment to start a project of this nature, for, in the summer of the following year, the tercentennial of Champlain's discovery of the lake that bears his name was to be celebrated. This was to be a most ambitious affair, with President Taft in attendance and some $150,000 appropriated for various celegrations up and down the lake.

Pell's first problem was to acquire the land from the many Pell heirs and to evict or buy off the numerous squatters who had pre-empted parts of the fort grounds. By this time, there were seventeen heirs to be dealt with, but this was successfully accomplished, and work was started on the West Barracks early in 1909. Scores of men were put to work cleaning away debris and then repairing and rebuilding the walls of the old building. Meanwhile, the Pavilion was being refurbished and made practical for modern living, a major accomplishment itself in view of the time available. On July 4, the Pavilion was ready to receive its distinguished guests, even though the furniture had arrived by canal boat only the day before. Save for its final tile roofing, the West Barracks were also essentially complete, and there was much to show the party of distinguished guests that accompanied the President. It was a most successful dedication of the rebirth of the fort.

During the next few years, Pell continued to enjoy the life of New York society, with winters either in the city or at Tuxedo

Stephen Hyatt Pelham Pell

Park and summers at Fort Ticonderoga. The fort was still a rich man's plaything, and far from being a lodestone to the traveling public. During this period, visitors, other than friends and house guests, were not overly encouraged. This was to come only with later years. Indeed, until the day of the motorcar, the fort was rather inaccessible to most people.

World War I was to mark the end of an era and disrupt many lives, among them that of Stephen Pell. The collapse of the stock market, resulting from the start of the war, ended Pell's activities in Wall Street. Fortunately, despite the crash, he was able to liquidate the company successfully. After a short hiatus in his active life, he enlisted in the Norton Harjes Ambulance Service, early in 1917, cheerfully lying about his age. He served that year with the French Army, becoming a sergeant and winning the Croix de Guerre. He was attached to the Chasseurs Alpins and proudly wore their little blue beret, which he treasured more than his Croix de Guerre. Late in 1917, he transferred to the American Army, where he accepted reduction to the rank of corporal without complaint. A friend who served with him at the front said that Stephen under shellfire was always cheerful, telling jokes and doing his best to boost the morale of his companions. In August, 1918, he was wounded and so ended his active career in France. Although one would not have expected it, Stephen Pell was a poet and, while in France, wrote some excellent verse.

After he returned from the war, Pell was at loose ends. He had little desire to go back into stockbroking or real estate, and so he let his always exuberant interest turn back to Ticonderoga. For the rest of his days, the old fort was to be his life. New construction required funds far beyond his personal ability to provide, but somehow money slowly trickled in from various sources. New exhibits were acquired for the museum, and additional reconstruction was undertaken from time to time. One of the great difficulties was the securing of cannon to arm the

Keepers of the Past

fort, and these were sought in all directions from Europe to the West Indies. The *New Yorker,* in February, 1931, reported that Stephen and two fellow members of the Union Club, years previously, had stolen two cannon to add to the fort's collection. That seems highly unlikely, but he might well have done it for a lark and left a check behind.

While Stephen was in France, so many visitors had come to the fort that Mrs. Pell was forced to hire a caretaker, and she then instituted a small admission charge to pay his wages. Hitherto, the fort and its grounds had been a private estate, but now the change into a public institution was starting to take place, and from this time on, visitors flocked to Ticonderoga in ever-increasing numbers. Upon Stephen's return from overseas, he installed a wartime comrade, Milo King, as manager of the fort. The two were to work together for nearly thirty years in furthering the restoration of the fort and in building the museum's collection.

In 1931, The Fort Ticonderoga Association was formed under the laws of the State of New York, and the entire property, fort, land, and museum, was donated by Stephen and Sarah to this non-profit, educational institution. Stephen was elected president and served for the rest of his life. He was succeeded by his son John, who today heads the corporation.

Sarah Pell died in 1939, and the fort became even more Stephen Pell's entire life. During the winter, he lived at his club, but early every spring, he moved to Ticonderoga and remained there until the fort closed in the fall. One of his pleasures was to sit in a chair at the entrance of the fort and refuse admission to ladies he felt were inadequately clothed. If his standards were applied today visitors would be few indeed! Stephen also took great pleasure in personally counting the money taken in admission charges, for the fort had no endowment and all maintenance and improvements were dependent upon collection of the admission charge. Thus he lived for some ten years, spending the winters collecting for the museum, seeking funds for further reconstruction, and awaiting the time when he could return again to his loved fort.

Stephen Pell was a great mixer; he could, it would seem, get along with anyone. He entered into the life of the Ticonderoga community and was much liked by the local people. Anyone who showed a real interest in the fort was at once his friend. An aristocrat, an economic royalist, and a hard-shell tory, he was a delight to all who knew him. Pell was a brilliant conversationalist and could always produce an apt story. He was strong in his beliefs and did not hesitate to express them. Only a sheet of asbestos paper could have held his comments on Franklin D. Roosevelt.

Unfortunately, Pell did not believe in keeping many records, and he destroyed the carbon copies of most of his letters, so today there is much that we do not know of the details of his life and of the restoration of Fort Ticonderoga. He did, however, take great pleasure in keeping voluminous scrapbooks, largely of newspaper clippings concerning the fort and the doings of the various members of the Pell family.

In his later years, Stephen was the recipient of many honors for his work in restoring the old fortress. The French Republic added the Legion of Honor to his war-won Croix de Guerre, and he was awarded honorary degrees by Norwich, Middlebury, and Union colleges. Vice president of both the New-York Historical Society and the New York State Historical Association, he was also active in many patriotic and genealogical societies.

Stephen Pell died in 1950 and was buried at the edge of the garden lying between the Pavilion and the walls of his beloved fort, a monument that, thanks to his efforts, stands today the same proud bastion that once dominated a whole sector of a continent.

John D. Rockefeller, Jr.

by Fairfield Osborn

~~~~~~~~~~~~~~~~~~~~~~~~~~

No inquiry concerned with human life is more fascinating than the attempt to discover the underlying motives of an individual's actions. This is true with any individual, even one whose life, like that of the great majority, is not marked by any notable characteristic or accomplishment. But when the rare person appears whose actions are evidently the result of unusual talents, combined with strong compulsions and beliefs, the effort to identify causes become doubly exciting. Such an attempt may prove baffling or even fruitless because the motivations involved in any person's actions are complex and often indefinable.

There is another aspect to all this. How can we explain great and unusual talents? The occasional "genius" may spring from apparently sterile soil—the gifted artist from a background of drab mediocrity, the great adventurer or explorer from a family of settled townfolk. Hidden lines of heredity are no doubt involved, latent within the individual and susceptible to some explosive incident that will mold all the after years.

In the case of John D. Rockefeller, Jr., it is evident that the influences to which he was exposed during his youth were of large importance throughout his lifetime—a foundation from which many of his actions emanated—but these were enriched

John D. Rockefeller, Jr

by sensitivities and conceptions that were his alone. His father was a man of unique capacities who, in the hard world of business competition, succeeded in amassing one of the world's great fortunes while he was still relatively young; it is frequently forgotten that the father ceased his activities in "money-making" at the age of fifty-four. During the next forty-odd years of his life, he gave himself to "contemplative" pursuits, if such they can be called. Principally, he occupied his acute mind with devising ways and means through which his wealth could benefit others. His thoughts turned mainly towards the great needs of health and education, and in these fields, he initiated programs that have since been of far-reaching and continuing benefit to people throughout the world.

One interest especially appealed to the son who, throughout the decades to come, was to carry it to a fruition never before approached—the preservation of natural and historical heritages. Reflecting a comparable interest in the beauties of nature, the father had written in his "Reminiscences," "How many miles of roads I have laid out in my time, I can hardly compute, but I have often kept at it until I was exhausted...." He comments with enthusiasm on the "pleasure and satisfaction of moving large trees" and with gratification on the rewards of "planning for good views." His goal was to recast the rolling hills of his property at Tarrytown into the rural aspect of the farmlands of Colonial days.

In the early years, father and son shared another common interest. They worked together in an endeavor to benefit the human, spiritual, and cultural values of the community in which they lived, aiding in the building of an adequate school and of the community church. It is especially notable that at a time when sectarianism was so general, they encouraged the creation of the local "Society for Christian Work" that included people of all denominations and creeds. Later, this was organized into the Union Church of Pocantico Hills. These earlier influences and enthusiasms endured and gave rise to the remarkable accomplishments of the son in later years.

Another aspect of the son's early life should be mentioned. Although his mother was an ardent fundamentalist, he evolved his own conception, which he thought of as the trinity of God, Man, and Nature. In religious matters, he believed strongly in the values to be gained through the coalescence of denominations and creeds, and a similar point of view governed his thoughts regarding international questions. As time went on, many of his benefactions were directed towards bringing concord among peoples of different races and nations. In his last years, the culmination of his efforts in this direction was realized by providing the funds needed to purchase the site for the United Nations in New York.

In contrast with those individuals to whom beauty has limited appeal and to whom the values of the past are dim or meaningless, this man had a passionate love of beauty—of the arts of nature as well as the arts of man. Of the Teton Mountains in Wyoming, he wrote: "Quite the grandest and most spectacular mountains I have ever seen . . . a picture of everchanging beauty which is to me beyond compare." As an illustration of the range of his tastes, he said of some pieces of old English china that were offered for sale to Colonial Williamsburg, "If Williamsburg doesn't care to acquire them, I shall, and if need be would put them in a closet until some time when I have a proper place for them and could enjoy their beauty."

While he innately was one to control his judgments, avoiding the pitfall of obsession with an idea, he yet considered it a "tragedy" that man took so little to heart and learned so infrequently from the experiences of the past. This conviction accounted for his extending aid towards the restoration and preservation of areas of historical significance. Here, too, he followed his belief in the values of internationalism, providing funds to aid the restoration of Versailles and Fontainebleau in

John D. Rockefeller, Jr.

France, supporting programs to discover and unearth the historical treasures of ancient Egypt, and encouraging similar efforts in other lands. So it was that the creation of Colonial Williamsburg was no whim, nor was it the consequence of a capricious idea, but the result of the conviction that the people of our country, their minds exclusively in the present, would gain a clearer vision of the meaning of our nation if they were aware of the factors that influenced its early history.

Although there is general awareness of his many benefactions, it is well to recall a number of them in order to illuminate the manner in which he pursued and attained his objectives. Obviously he was subject to innumerable appeals for "good causes," and, although for special reasons he responded to many, the fact remained that he constantly kept in mind the specific directions in which he considered his wealth could best be applied for the benefit of his fellow countrymen and people of other lands. Time will justify these decisions, for they will endure into the long future.

Whether he foresaw the course of events or whether the choices he made early in life have merely justified themselves cannot be determined—one may well believe it was a combination of the two. As the years pass, what he has done in establishing, in permanent form, historical and natural landmarks in his own country and abroad is proving of ever greater significance. Even now, only a few years after his death, our nation is becoming sharply conscious of the degrading consequences of our onrushing civilization—ever greater numbers of people, the disappearance of open spaces, the deadening sameness of the urban sprawl, the pollution of air and waterways, the gray monotony of concrete where once the oak groves stood. Fortunately, present concern has become so acute that there is promise of a turning of this evil tide. The federal government and a number of state governments are taking action, largely as a result of this ever-increasing public concern. At best, the remedies will only follow

Keepers of the Past

long years of struggle and effort, for the difficulties are many and varied, and their solutions are not easily attainable. Meanwhile, unhappily, the tide continues to run its calamitous course.

Yet this one man, many years ago, took upon himself the task of counteracting the serious trends that have now become so evident. In doing this, he made possible, often singlehandedly, the establishment of what may be considered the bulwarks against a tide of destruction—superb natural regions as well as precious historical sites that will last through time and change. His accomplishments were of extraordinary scope and magnitude, and they extend throughout our country. Among them are the preservation of the Palisades of the Hudson in New York, the development of the Palisades Interstate Park to the north, and the preservation of several historical sites in the lower Hudson River Valley at Philipsburg Manor, Van Cortlandt Manor, and Washington Irving's "Sunnyside," all richly expressive of the early days of our country. To New York City he gave Fort Tryon Park and financed the construction of The Cloisters, located within the park, as well as making possible the purchase of medieval sculpture and architecture that The Cloisters contains.

His interests then began to reach beyond the vicinity of Tarrytown, and he became convinced of the great need for more national parks while land was still available for their creation. Without his vision and assistance, four superb national parks in the United States would presumably never have come into existence—the Acadia in Maine, the Shenandoah in the Blue Ridge Mountains of Virginia, the Great Smoky Mountains in the Appalachian Range within Tennessee and North Carolina, and the Grand Teton National Park in Wyoming. He also aided in the extension of Yosemite National Park, the acquisition of Redwood Groves in California, and, in the last years of his life, with his son Laurance, in the creation of the Virgin Islands National Park.

John D. Rockefeller, Jr.

It might be thought that a life such as this, filled with accomplishment and riches, would be free of the anxieties and disappointments common in the life of "everyman." There is no question that he gained much satisfaction. Often, too, he was able to respond to deep emotions within himself, as illustrated by the wish he expressed in connection with his gift to the Great Smoky Mountains National Park, that it stand as "a memorial to the beautiful spirit of my mother." Again, it must have been with profound happiness that he witnessed the development of Colonial Williamsburg, most notable and influential of historical restorations. When he made possible the long-term protection of beautiful things, whether the art of nature or the art of man, he must have experienced a great inner joy.

Despite all of this, he had troubles peculiar to a man in his position. Those who worked intimately with him say that he thought of his money, having come largely from his father, as a sacred trust that had to be used for the betterment of mankind. This created in him an ever-present sense of responsibility, and there were other concerns that sometimes must have been hard to bear. As might be expected, some of his actions prompted controversies and criticisms that caused him considerable unhappiness. One instance concerned the creation of the Grand Teton National Park. The great majority of the landowners most willingly accepted the fair prices offered for their property, but after several years, when some thirty thousand acres had been acquired, a bitter and primarily political controversy arose in which an opposition faction desperately fought the plan to have the property come under the federal government and thus become a national park for the people of the entire nation. This controversy lasted some twenty years and must have called for great patience and forbearance on the part of the man whose only objective was the greatest public good.

There is a saying that "the capacity for taking infinite pains" is a mark of genius. If this observation has validity, such a measure of competence can justifiably be applied to this man who was indefatigable in the time and study he applied to every element of the plans and projects in which he became engaged. One can surmise that he felt deeply that money was not all and that he must give of himself.

Several years ago I was given the privilege of writing a brief foreword to a book entitled *A Contribution to the Heritage of Every American,* which dealt in considerable detail with his accomplishments in conservation and the restoration of historical landmarks. This foreword included the following thoughts that may serve to summarize what has been expressed here:

> These things were not easily done. Vision alone was not enough. Wealth alone was insufficient. Concept of the plan as a whole, arduous attention to detail and even passion for perfection, feeling for color and beauty, respect for working associates, talent for administration, patience and, lastly, tolerance of criticism and even of misunderstanding of purpose—all these qualities were brought into play, for all were essential to the fulfillment of the early vision.
>
> How can these contributions to the life of the people of the United States be measured? It is not enough to say that at this very time over fifty million visits are made each year by Americans as well as people from far countries, gaining recreation, knowledge and inspiration in these places that are the result of his dedication. The years will roll on. Ever greater numbers of people will find benefit to body and spirit in these shrines of nature and history. Thus the vision remains, but it is beyond the mind of man to measure the essences that are the heritage of every American.

The Authors

L. ROBERT ABLES is currently on leave as associate professor of social sciences from Amarillo College, Texas, working as a teaching assistant at the University of Texas while completing his doctoral studies.

JAMES F. DOSTER, professor of history at the University of Alabama, became acquainted with the Alabama Department of Archives and History when working there on his doctoral dissertation for the University of Chicago. Alabama born, he has taught at the University of Alabama since 1936, specializing in railroad history.

JAMES TAYLOR FORREST, director of the Bradford Brinton Memorial, Big Horn, Wyoming, served both the Wisconsin and Colorado Historical Societies, and is a former director of both the Gilcrease Institute of American History and Art and the Museum of New Mexico. He holds his doctorate from the University of Wisconsin.

LARRY GARA, is associate professor of history and government at Wilmington College, Ohio. He has taught in colleges in Illinois, Mexico, Pennsylvania, and Delaware, and is the author of four books. He was research assistant to the late William B. Hesseltine when Hesseltine was writing the biography of Lyman Copeland Draper, and he holds his doctorate from the University of Wisconsin.

The Authors

EDWARD P. HAMILTON, a graduate of Harvard, trained as an engineer but later shifted his interests to investment management. He served as an artilleryman in both world wars, rising to the rank of colonel. He has been director of Fort Ticonderoga since 1957 and is the author of several books on the colonial period.

JAMES J. HESLIN, director of the New-York Historical Society, holds the doctorate in history from Boston University and a library degree from Columbia University. He was assistant director of university libraries at the University of Buffalo before coming to the New-York Historical Society.

CHARLES B. HOSMER, JR., is assistant professor of history at Principia College and holds the doctorate in history from Teachers College, Columbia University. His *Presence of the Past: A History of the Preservation Movement in the United States before Williamsburg* has just been published by the National Trust for Historic Preservation.

JOHN ALLEN KROUT has served his alma mater, Columbia University, in every academic rank from instructor in history to dean of the graduate faculties, provost and vice-president. He presently is acting dean of Heidelberg College, Ohio.

HUGH T. LEFLER is Kenan Professor of history at the University of North Carolina, holds his doctorate from the University of Pennsylvania, and is the author of some twenty books, half of them on North Carolina.

G. CARROLL LINDSAY, after graduating from Dickinson School of Law, Carlisle, Pennsylvania, became a Fellow of the Winterthur Program in Early American Culture. He stayed on for one year as assistant to the director of the Winterthur Museum and then joined the Smithsonian, where he has been curator of the Museum Service since 1958.

BERTRAM K. LITTLE is director of the Society for the Preservation of New England Antiquities, a post to which he was attracted after some eighteen years in book and magazine

The Authors

publishing. A productive author, he is also active in a number of historical societies, preservation groups, and collectors' clubs, including the American Antiquarian Society, the Massachusetts Historical Society, the Colonial Society of Massachusetts, and the Walpole Society.

CLIFFORD L. LORD, president of Hofstra University, has served as director of both the New York State Historical Association and the State Historical Society of Wisconsin, as president of the American Association for State and Local History, and as dean of the Faculty of General Studies at Columbia University.

FAIRFIELD OSBORN is president of the New York Zoological Society and chairman of the Conservation Foundation. A distinguished conservationist, his writings and speeches have won him many honors and international recognition.

JOHN E. POMFRET is director of the Huntington Library and Art Gallery, San Marino, California, has taught at Princeton, served as dean of the senior college and graduate school at Vanderbilt University, and (1942-51) as president of the College of William and Mary. He is a cofounder of the Institute of Early American History and Culture at Williamsburg.

STEPHEN T. RILEY did both his undergraduate and graduate work at Clark University. After receiving his doctorate, he joined the staff of the Massachusetts Historical Society and became director in 1957.

DAVID D. VAN TASSEL is professor of history at the University of Texas. His most recent book is a history of the American Historical Association. He, too, is a Wisconsin Ph.D.

www.ingramcontent.com/pod-product-compliance
Lightning Source LLC
Chambersburg PA
CBHW021401290426
44108CB00010B/337